Common Sense Safety for Women

We Can Learn to Live Safely as Mothers, Wives, and Business Professionals in a Man's World!

Using Common Sense for Self-Defense

Joanne Morin Correia

Table of Contents

It is Personal 4

Combating the Crisis of Violence for Women in the US 10

Women are VERY Fearful 15

Empowerment Requires Mental & Physical Self-Defense Training 23

Avoiding Abduction 33

The Mind of Predators 39

Seconds Matter 53

Understanding Self-Defense Laws 61

Home Safety Tips 72

On Road Safety 90

Traveling is not the Time to Let Your Guard Down 95

Distraction Crimes 106

Compliance 112

Protect Your Financial Accounts 116

Cyberbullying is Not a Problem Just for Children 126

Online Dating Can Be a Positive Experience 130

Use What You Got 145

Weapons On Your Body 156

Summary Posters for Printing or Sharing 172

....
Error! Bookmark not defined.

References – Books and Websites 196

Biography 201

It is Personal

As a child in the 60s, my best friend Stephen was molested by our guitar teacher on Main Street in Enfield. Ct. When they tried to get me to join them, I ran out of the Music Store and hid in the Catholic church across the street. I feared what I had witnessed, and I did not understand what was happening to my best friend. I didn't tell anyone to move to a different school away from Stephen at the end of the school year. We didn't discuss those things back then.

In the mid-1970s, while in high school, Stephen and I worked at the same department store, GFOX, in the mall. He sat next to me, waiting for a ride, and tried to talk to me about what had happened seven years earlier. I couldn't open that door, and I walked away; he committed suicide that night.

It wasn't until my Forties, when I was in the radKIDs.org's Instructor Training in Sturbridge, Mass., that I finally came to terms with not talking about it when we were training the kids. They need to talk about things when Adults tell them not to, or something bad will happen.

I dedicate this book to Stephen, as he was unaware of the impact of this predictor on him. We need to discuss this to protect our children and others. I wish I had known this that evening and given him more support.

During the late 70s, I went to Bermuda for a College Week of Fun. I rented an apartment with two other women and hung around with a long-time male friend, thinking I would be safer. All week, we danced to a Band called the Bermuda Strollers.

The lead singer asked me on stage to dance several times during the week, and I saw him a few times around the apt. On the final night, he asked me if I would like a tour of the island before I flew home, and if I wanted to see other apartments in case I wanted to return. I said yes.

At his apartment, there were several men, and he pushed me into a bedroom, where there were several knives on the table. He raped me as I pretended to cooperate (I worked for Planned Parenthood, and we were told rapists usually do not murder their victims). Then he took me to the airport, and I boarded my plane to return to Boston. He called me a few years later for a date.

In the 1980s, I traveled the world as a Marketing Manager for Digital Corporation. I had some issues with being followed back to my hotel room and concerns about taxi drivers getting me to my destination. There were no travel-safe guides or mentors available to speak with, which could have helped make it safer. I used my gut, wit, and lessons learned as a tomboy to stay safe.

In the '90s, I was at an IBM event in San Francisco at a "closed" mall with a fantastic band; my male business partner, John, did not want to stay. I told him to leave, and I would taxi back and meet him in the morning.

In less than an hour, I felt like I was going to black out, so I said to the person I was hanging with, I do not feel right, and I headed to the ladies' room. I blacked out before I was able to close the stall door and woke up @30 minutes later; I was date drugged. The ladies helped me get a taxi, and I returned safely to the hotel.

I began my Taekwondo training in my forties and earned my Black Belt at the age of 50. I also trained as an instructor with RAD and radKIDS, teaching over 1,000 students, including my children, friends, and family, through Common Sense Safety Classes and Rouleau-Holley's Martial Arts.

Our daughter, Jess, was on a Cruise with us and was Date Rape Drugged while she was in a "Safe" Teenage area. She knew enough to get back to us, so several friends on the boat took her to our room.

I watched her go through the stages of being drugged; I called the Doctor on board, and he said, "It was unfortunate, and there was Nothing he could do," but to make sure she did not stop breathing.

On another trip, in broad daylight, Jess was followed, grabbed, and then managed to escape, only to be chased by two men in London, England. She ran into the lobby of a Marriott hotel, and the men turned around and fled. She had the bellman call a taxi for her to return to our hotel, which was several blocks away.

Thankfully, I had trained her to get out of a grab, know where to run, and how to return safely to me, as I had given her taxi money just in case. Jess was also a member of the Cross-Country Team.

At night, sometimes, I replay in my mind the women and children telling their 1,000s of stories of survival when men and women tried to do unspeakable things to them. We taught hundreds of them in our classes as they were filled with children from 3 to 16, foster children, nurses, case workers, teachers, wives, cult escapers, realtors, domestic abuse and rape survivors, and yes, murder witnesses.

Our goal was to make them feel safer despite what had happened. But things changed with the school shootings and other mass shootings. This changes the entire safety scenario because it is unpredictable and aggressive. The authorities often do not know what they do not know or listen to witnesses, and as a result, they fail to act and cannot prevent the violence.

However, there are many good men and women who can make a significant difference in addressing this safety issue. I alone cannot change the world to make it a safer and kinder place.

We can help people learn to rely on their common sense and instincts to be safer while they enjoy their lives, despite what has happened to them.

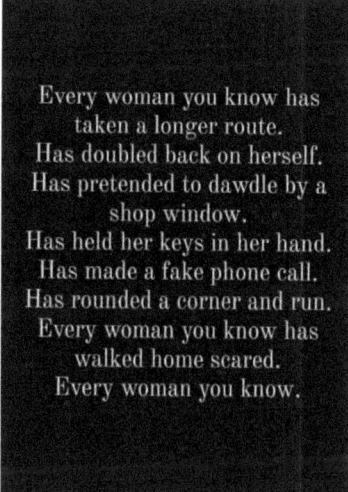

Thank you for putting up with me.

This journey would not have happened without the love and support of my Husband, Joe, my best friend. Throughout the decades of trying to save the world, I have brought to our "safe" home: horses, dogs, cats, seagulls, and people — women and teenagers just trying to survive.

To our children, Jessica (Jess) and Jonathan (Jon), who trained and taught with me for years. We learned a lot together and helped many people stay safer.

To my manager at Info-Tech, Dave, who supported me by listening to me. And to my friends Shar, Marijane, Sandy, Cat, and others who have helped support me through the multiple versions of this book.

To the martial arts instructors and friends from **R+H Taekwondo Do,** including Senesi Rouleau, Senesi Buzby, and our radKIDs team of Stephanie and Christine, for encouraging us to instruct children and women in the **RAD Systems of Defense** and **radKIDS.**

Combating the Crisis of Violence for Women in the US

End the Stereotypes & Normalization of Violence

All Images generated by OpenAI's DALL·E [Large language model] (2024 & 2025) unless noted

Living as a woman in America through the 1970s, '80s, and '90s was fraught with danger. Domestic violence was routinely treated as a private family matter, financial dependence on husbands left women with few options for escape, and the law offered minimal protection—marital rape wasn't even recognized as a crime until the 1990s. Over subsequent decades, landmark reforms like the Violence Against Women Act, the criminalization of marital rape, more vigorous restraining-order enforcement, and growing economic opportunities began to chip away at those risks.

Business travel for women in the 1980s and 1990s carried its perils: rampant sexual harassment, discrimination in hotels and taxis, and the absence of cell phones or online support networks to call for help. Today's in-flight safety briefings, 24/7 hotlines, and smartphone apps for lone travelers all grew out of those hard-won lessons.

Yet with President Trump's return to the White House, many of those gains are suddenly under threat. Conservative rollbacks of key VAWA provisions, renewed challenges to reproductive rights, and pandemic-era strains on social services have combined to plunge women's safety into a full-blown national crisis.

Reversals of legal protections and cuts to healthcare and domestic-violence funding now demand an urgent, coordinated response: beefed-up legal enforcement, restored reproductive and mental-health access, workplace training on harassment, and renewed investment in shelters and advocacy networks.

Without swift action, decades of progress risk being undone, and far too many women will again find home and work in dangerous places.

It is a Crisis

Across the United States, women's safety varies widely by issue and geography. Nationally, one in four women will experience severe intimate partner violence, and one in five will face completed or attempted rape during her lifetime. In 2020, roughly 2,000 women were murdered — over half by an intimate partner — and one in six women have been stalked.

Human trafficking disproportionately affects women and girls, with hotspots in major corridors such as California, Texas, and Florida.

Yet these risks are far from uniform: Alaska's rates of domestic and sexual violence can double the national average, while states like New York and Massachusetts report substantially lower homicide and assault figures.

Understanding these patterns by analyzing statistics — both at the national level and in their state-by-state nuances — is crucial to targeting prevention, support, and policy interventions where they are most needed.

Category	National Statistic	State Variation (Examples)
Domestic Violence	1 in 4 women have experienced severe intimate partner violence (CDC)	Alaska: ~50% of women New York: ~25% of women
Sexual Violence	1 in 5 women have experienced completed or attempted rape	Alaska: ~59 incidents per 100,000 New Jersey/Connecticut: ~22–25 incidents per 100,000
Homicide	~2,000 women murdered in 2020; over half by an intimate partner (FBI)	Louisiana: ~2.6 homicides per 100,000 women Massachusetts: ~0.9 homicides per 100,000 women
Stalking	1 in 6 women has been stalked	West Virginia/North Dakota: ~18% of women
Human Trafficking	Women and girls make up most trafficking victims	California: >1,000 cases reported annually High prevalence also in Texas and Florida

Data sources include the CDC's National Intimate Partner and Sexual Violence Survey (NISVS), FBI Uniform Crime Reporting (UCR), and the National Coalition Against Domestic Violence (NCADV).

Women are VERY Fearful

Roots of Fear, Urgent Need for Cultural and Social Reforms.

Women today often experience a heightened sense of fear due to a combination of social and psychological factors. Historical and ongoing threats of violence, personal experiences, and social conditioning contribute to this pervasive fear, as women have been conditioned to be cautious to avoid becoming victims of male violence. Trust issues further exacerbate this fear, as the intentions of unknown men are seen as unpredictable and potentially dangerous.

Cultural narratives and media representations also amplify these fears by frequently highlighting stories of male-perpetrated violence. This complex interplay of factors is vividly illustrated in the current social media discussion about whether women prefer to encounter a bear or an unknown man in the woods. This hypothetical scenario, which has garnered significant attention on platforms like TikTok, underscores the deep-seated fears many women have regarding male violence. It highlights the need for societal changes to address and reduce gender-based violence, ensuring women's safety and security in all aspects of life.

Women today often feel a heightened sense of fear due to a variety of social and psychological factors. Studies and social discussions reveal several reasons why women might feel this way and why some even choose hypothetical scenarios involving dangerous animals over encounters with unknown men.

Reasons for Increased Fear:

- **Ongoing Threat of Violence:** Women have long been conditioned to be wary of potential violence from men due to high rates of domestic violence, sexual assault, and harassment. This historical context contributes to an ingrained sense of caution and fear.

- **Personal Experiences and Social Conditioning:** Many women have personal or second-hand experiences of male violence, which reinforces the fear of unknown men. Social conditioning teaches women to be vigilant and cautious to avoid becoming victims.

- **Trust Issues:** There is a general mistrust of unknown men because a bear's intentions are perceived as straightforward and predictable, whereas a man's intentions are seen as uncertain and potentially dangerous.

- **Cultural Narratives and Media Representation:** The Media often highlight stories of male-perpetrated violence, which can amplify fears. These narratives contribute to a culture where women feel constantly on guard against potential threats from men.

The current discussion about whether women would prefer to encounter a bear or an unknown man in the woods highlights the deep-seated fears many women have regarding male violence.

This hypothetical scenario, which has garnered significant attention and responses on social media platforms like TikTok, reveals that many women feel safer facing a bear because the animal's behavior is seen as predictable compared to the potential threat posed by a man. The bear is perceived as a straightforward danger, whereas an unknown man represents an unpredictable risk of violence, harassment, or assault. This choice underscores the extent of distrust and fear that women harbor due to personal experiences and societal conditioning, where the potential for male violence is ever-present.

The widespread resonance of this hypothetical question, which was explored through a series of interviews and discussions on social media, highlights the urgent need for societal changes to address and reduce gender-based violence and ensure women's safety and security in all aspects of life.

The fear many women experience today is a complex interplay of personal experiences, social conditioning, and cultural narratives. It underscores the broader issue of gender-based violence and the need for societal changes to ensure women feel safe and secure in their daily lives.

TRAUMA RESPONSES

FLIGHT
- Workaholic
- Over-thinker
- Anxiety, panic, OCD
- Difficulty sitting still
- Perfectionist

FIGHT
- Anger outburst
- Controlling
- "The bully"
- Narcissistic
- Explosive behaviour

FREEZE
- Difficulty making decisions
- Stuck
- Dissociation
- Isolating
- Numb

FAWN
- People pleaser
- Lack of identity
- No boundaries
- Overwhelmed
- Codependent

@RYANTHEHOLISTICHEALTHCOACH

Use Fear for Survival

One of my favorite books is "The Gift of Fear: Survival Signals That Protect Us from Violence" by Gavin de Becker, which emphasizes the importance of trusting one's instincts and intuition as powerful tools for personal safety. Here are the key takeaways and learnings from the book:

- **Trust Your Instincts:** De Becker argues that intuition is a powerful survival mechanism that can protect us from harm. He stresses the importance of listening to gut feelings and internal warnings, as these are often based on subtle cues that our subconscious picks up on.

- **Understanding Fear:** Fear is a natural and valuable emotion that signals danger. The book teaches readers to distinguish between genuine fear — a response to immediate threats — and unwarranted anxiety — a response to perceived, but not confirmed, threats.

- **Pre-Incident Indicators:** De Becker identifies behaviors and signals often preceding violence, such as forced teaming, charm, and excessive detail. Recognizing these pre-incident indicators can help individuals identify and avoid potentially dangerous situations.

- **Survival Signals:** The book outlines specific signals and behaviors that can alert someone to danger.
    - **Forced Teaming:** An attempt to create a false sense of unity or partnership.
    - **Charm and Niceness:** Used manipulatively to disarm and gain trust.
    - **Too Many Details:** Over-explaining to convince someone of something untrue.
    - **Typecasting:** Using a slight insult to make someone prove their worth.
    - **Loan Sharking**: Offering unsolicited help to create a sense of obligation.
    - **The Unsolicited Promise:** Promising something without being asked, often to gain trust.
    - **Discounting the Word "No":** Not accepting boundaries is a major red flag.

- **Real-Life Examples:** The book features numerous real-life examples and case studies that illustrate how intuition and awareness have saved lives. These stories reinforce the practical application of the concepts discussed.

"The Gift of Fear" is a powerful reminder that our intuition and instincts are crucial tools for survival. By learning to trust and act on these internal signals, individuals can better protect themselves from violence and harm. De Becker's insights into the behaviors that precede violence, along with his practical advice for personal safety, make this book an essential read for anyone interested in improving their situational awareness and security.

Empowerment Requires Mental & Physical Self-Defense Training

Address Societal Gaps in Training & Survival Skills

Traditional self-defense training often focuses on physical combat, which can be less effective for women facing stronger male attackers. These classes may overlook real-world scenarios that require situational awareness and psychological readiness, both of which are crucial for actual encounters.

Additionally, limited self-defense training can create a false sense of security, leading individuals to take unnecessary risks.

In contrast, survival training encompasses a broader range of skills, including situational awareness, risk avoidance, and emergency planning, which are essential for overall safety.

Societal Failures in Training Women

- **Cultural Norms**: From a young age, girls are socialized to be passive and non-confrontational, often prioritizing politeness and compliance over assertiveness. This socialization can hinder their ability to defend themselves effectively in dangerous situations.

- **Education:** Schools and educational programs rarely include self-defense or survival training in their curricula. Physical education typically emphasizes traditional sports over practical self-defense skills, leaving girls without essential tools for personal safety.

- **Access and Encouragement**: Women may face fewer opportunities to engage in self-defense training due to societal discouragement, financial barriers, and a lack of accessible programs. These obstacles perpetuate the notion that women are incapable of defending themselves.

- **Victim-Blaming**: Society often focuses on what women should do to avoid being attacked, such as not walking alone at night, rather than empowering them with skills to protect themselves in any situation. This shifts the responsibility onto women to avoid dangerous situations instead of addressing the root causes of violence.

- **Media Representation:** The Media frequently portrays women as victims rather than capable defenders. This lack of positive representation can impact women's perceptions of their abilities and erode their confidence in handling challenging situations.

Improving Training for Women

- **Early Education**: Incorporating self-defense and situational awareness training into school curricula can help build these essential skills from a young age, empowering girls to protect themselves effectively.

- **Positive Role Models**: Highlighting stories and media portrayals of women successfully defending themselves can inspire and empower others, showing that women can effectively protect themselves.

- **Accessible Programs:** Offering self-defense programs that are affordable and inclusive for all women can increase participation and ensure that more women can learn these vital skills.
- **Supportive Environment:** Encouraging a culture that supports and values training for women can help break down stereotypes and societal norms that discourage such training, fostering a more inclusive and empowering environment.

Physical Education and Sports

- **Gender Stereotypes:** Physical education often reinforces traditional gender roles, with boys encouraged to participate in competitive and aggressive sports while girls are steered towards less intense activities. This can limit girls' opportunities to develop strength and confidence.

- **Unequal Opportunities:** Girls require more opportunities and encouragement to participate in sports, which can lead to lower physical fitness and self-esteem. This disparity can perpetuate the notion that girls' physical prowess is less important.

- **Body Image Issues:** The societal focus on physical appearance can impact girls more severely, leading to self-consciousness and a reluctance to engage in physical activities fully. Boys are generally encouraged to value strength and athleticism more, positively influencing their engagement in sports.

- **Lack of Role Models:** The scarcity of female role models in many sports can discourage girls from participating. Conversely, boys often see numerous male athletes celebrated in the media, boosting their involvement and confidence.

- **Perceived Physical Abilities:** Girls may internalize societal messages that they are less capable physically, which can affect their performance and participation in sports. In contrast, boys often receive reinforcement for their physical abilities, which boosts their confidence and engagement.

Recommendations for Improvement

- **Inclusive Curriculum**: Develop a physical education curriculum that promotes equality, encouraging both boys and girls to participate in a range of activities.

- **Encourage Participation:** Actively support and encourage girls to engage in sports from a young age, providing equal resources and opportunities.

- **Positive Role Models:** Highlight and celebrate female athletes to provide positive role models for girls, showing them that they can succeed in sports.

- **Body Positivity**: Foster a positive body image environment that emphasizes health and fitness over appearance, helping all students feel confident and motivated to participate in physical activities.

By addressing these issues, physical education can become a more inclusive and empowering experience for all students. It can help break down gender barriers and promote equal participation, bridging the Gap Between Self-Defense Training and Survival Skills to create a safer, More Confident Society.

Another one of my favorite books is Meditations on Violence: A Comparison of Martial Arts Training and Real-World Violence" by Rory Miller.

It discusses the gaps between martial arts training and the realities of actual violence. Miller, a seasoned corrections officer and martial artist, offers a comprehensive analysis of the psychological and physical aspects of violent encounters. He emphasizes the differences between dojo training and real-world situations, offering practical advice on how to respond to threats effectively.

The book covers topics such as attackers' mindsets, the effects of adrenaline, and the importance of situational awareness. It's a critical read for anyone interested in realistic self-defense training. What did I learn?

- **The Difference Between Training and Reality:** Traditional martial arts training often fails to simulate the unpredictability and chaos of real-world violence. Real encounters are more sudden, intense, and unstructured.

- **Mindset and Psychology:** Understanding attackers' mindsets and recognizing the effects of adrenaline are crucial. Mental preparation and situational awareness can be as important as physical skills.

- **Adaptability:** Techniques practiced in a controlled environment may need to be adapted or abandoned in a real fight. Flexibility and improvisation are key.

- **Realistic Training:** Incorporating scenario-based training that mimics real-life situations can better prepare individuals for actual confrontations.

- **Legal and Ethical Considerations**: Knowing the legal implications of self-defense actions and the ethical boundaries is essential. Understanding when and how to use force appropriately is also critical to self-defence.

These lessons emphasize the importance of realistic training and mental preparedness for effectively handling real-world violence. I suggest you look for realistic training scenarios at www.rad-systems.com, which offers training across the US and Canada.

Other Books and Resources on Self-Defense and Empowerment for Women
- **The New Superpower for Women**: Trust Your Intuition, Predict Dangerous Situations, and Defend Yourself from the Unthinkable, by Steve Kardian, teaches practical self-defense techniques to women, helping them harness their intuition.
- **When Violence Is the Answer**: Learning How to Do What It Takes When Your Life Is at Stake, by Tim Larkin, explores the mindset and techniques necessary for practical self-defence.

Online Resources
- **National Self-Defense Institute**: Provides self-defense and personal safety training and resources.
- **RAINN (Rape, Abuse & Incest National Network):** Offers information and support for victims of sexual violence.

These books and resources provide valuable insights into self-defence, situational awareness, and the psychological aspects of staying safe. They can help women build confidence and practical skills to protect themselves.

Avoiding Abduction

Be Alert, Stay Safe, and Prevent Dangerous Situations

Abduction is not just a standalone crime; it frequently precedes other severe offenses, making its prevention and immediate counteraction crucial for personal safety.

Many defense strategies are specifically designed to avoid or escape abduction scenarios, which are particularly relevant to women, as such strategies are generally less applicable to men.

Abduction can be defined as the act of forcibly taking someone away against their will.

This act not only restricts a person's freedom of movement but also creates a perilous situation where the victim is isolated and under the control of the abductor.

The methods used in abduction typically include:
- physical force
- threats of violence
- or psychological intimidation
- all aimed at overpowering the victim and preventing escape.

From a legal standpoint, abduction is treated as a severe crime (Felony) due to its implications and the potential for subsequent criminal activities, such as assault, sexual violence, or murder.

The crime of abduction, classified as a felony, often involves the unlawful restraint of a person's freedom of movement through force, threat, or intimidation.

In many jurisdictions, the legal system imposes harsh penalties on those convicted of abduction to deter such crimes and protect potential victims. Understanding the legal definitions and implications of abduction is crucial for recognizing the seriousness of the threat and the importance of taking defensive measures.

Avoiding abduction is a critical aspect of self-defence, as it significantly reduces the risk of further violence and harm. Once abducted, an individual loses control and faces heightened danger in isolated locations.

We need to emphasize that situational awareness, early escape, and effective self-defense techniques are among the most crucial measures for preventing abduction. By understanding and implementing these strategies, individuals can enhance their safety and be better prepared to respond to potential threats, ensuring they remain in control and minimize the risks associated with dangerous situations.

Avoiding Abduction is Key to Safety and Defense

- **Situational Awareness:** Remaining aware of your surroundings is crucial for avoiding abduction. This involves being vigilant, especially in unfamiliar or isolated areas.

- **Trust your instincts:** if something feels off, it probably is. Being observant and mindful can help you recognize potential threats early and take pre-emptive action to avoid danger.

- **Avoid Routine:** Predictability can make you an easier target for someone planning an abduction. By varying your routines and routes, you make it more difficult for a potential attacker to anticipate your movements and plan an attack. This unpredictability can significantly reduce the risk of being targeted.

- **Escape Early:** The best time to escape is during the initial moments of an attack, when attackers are often least prepared for resistance. Use any available means to create a distraction, such as throwing objects or making sudden movements, to increase your chances of breaking free and getting away before the situation escalates.

- **Make Noise:** Making noise can attract attention and deter an attacker. Scream, use a personal alarm, or bang on objects to create loud noises. The goal is to alert others nearby to your distress and scare off the attacker, who might not want to be aware of their actions.

- **Fight Back:** If escape isn't immediately possible, using 120% of your effort and techniques to fight back can be crucial. Target vulnerable areas of the attacker, such as the eyes, nose, throat, and groin, to inflict pain and create an opportunity to escape. Self-defense and situational training can help you learn how to handle such violent attacks.

- Implementing these strategies can enhance personal safety and reduce the likelihood of abduction. Staying aware, being prepared to escape or fight back, making noise, and avoiding predictable patterns are all essential elements of a robust self-defense plan.

I Fight Like a Girl

With a sense of anger and an unwavering will to fight back fiercely in a life-or-death struggle:

I fight like a girl, with fury unchained,
With fists that won't falter, with blood in my veins.
I am rage in the darkness, a storm that won't break,

For I'll fight to the death – I'm no easy take.

I fight like a girl, every breath charged with fire,
With wrath in my heart, with vengeance inspired.
I will claw, I will bite, I will tear to be free,
And death stands beside me, unyielding as I am.

I fight like a girl, and I won't go unheard,
With screams that cut deep, as sharp as my words.
My anger's my armor; my pulse beats like war,
I won't stop till I've won, till I'm safe, till you're gone.

I fight like a girl, with all that I am,
With power that terrifies, that no one can damn.
So if you come for me, know I'll answer with wrath,

For I fight like a girl – and I'll fight to the last.

Source: Circulates online as an anonymous or user-generated piece. There's no known author, publisher, or first appearance in a recognized collection.

The Mind of Predators

Recognize and Avoid Dangerous People

Predatory behavior is far more common than most people realize: studies estimate that one in five women and one in seventy-one men will experience sexual assault in their lifetime, and roughly 90% of those perpetrators are known friends, intimate partners, or acquaintances, rather than strangers!

Predators often scout for vulnerability, targeting those who appear isolated, distracted, or emotionally distressed. They move quickly—sometimes befriending a victim online or in person within hours—and employ tactics such as feigned sympathy, charm, or "tests" of trust to lower their victim's defenses.

While violent assaults grab headlines, most predator attacks involve gradual emotional manipulation, making early recognition of grooming behaviors (excessive flattery, unsolicited gifts, boundary-pushing questions) and situational red flags (requests for secrecy, attempts to isolate) critical.

By understanding that predatory tactics can unfold in minutes or span weeks—and that opportunistic predators look for both physical and online openings—women can stay more vigilant, trust their instincts, and employ protective strategies like setting firm boundaries, maintaining public meeting places, and using trusted "check-ins" with friends or family to disrupt a predator's plans before they escalate.

Predators use manipulative and deceptive tactics to target vulnerable individuals, making it essential to understand their behaviors and strategies.

The statistic that "more than 2 million women are assaulted every year" might have been relevant in the past. Still, current data suggests that the number of women experiencing intimate partner violence and sexual assault annually in the U.S. is significantly higher when considering physical assaults alongside sexual assaults.

Many incidents go unreported, making it challenging to determine the exact number of assaults. Here's a more current understanding of the issue:

- **Intimate Partner Violence:** The National Center for Injury Prevention and Control indicates that women experience about **4.8 million** intimate partner-related physical assaults and rapes every year.[1]

- **Lifetime Prevalence:** Approximately 1 in 5 (21.3% or an estimated **25.5 million**) women in the U.S. report experiencing completed or attempted rape at some point in their lifetime.

- **Broader Context:** Every year, nearly 10 million women and men become victims of domestic violence in the United States. Intimate partner violence accounts for 15% of all violent crime.

Let's examine the profiles, motivations, and methods of common predators, including their strategies for selecting and hunting victims. By recognizing these patterns and implementing proactive safety measures, women can significantly reduce their risk of becoming targets.

Tim Larkin, author of "Survive the Unthinkable: A Total Guide to Women's Self-Protection, believes that traditional self-defense training for women is not enough because it often focuses solely on physical techniques without addressing the broader context of violence and the mindset needed to prevent and respond to it effectively.

Here are some key reasons he provides, along with insights into the alarming statistics:

- **Mindset and Preparedness:** Larkin emphasizes that physical techniques alone are insufficient without the right mindset. Women need to be mentally prepared to recognize and react to threats before they escalate to physical violence.

    - **Insight:** Many women are not taught to trust their instincts or to be assertive in setting and maintaining boundaries, leaving them vulnerable to escalating situations.

- **Comprehensive Awareness**: Effective self-defense requires situational awareness and the ability to recognize and avoid potentially hazardous situations.

    - **Insight:** Traditional self-defense classes often need more time to teach women to be constantly aware of their surroundings and identify potential threats early.

- **Understanding the Attacker's Mindset:** Larkin stresses the importance of understanding how attackers think and operate. This knowledge can help women anticipate and thwart potential attacks.
    - **Insight:** Without this understanding, women may not fully grasp the importance of early intervention and proactive measures to prevent an attack.

- **Behavioral Strategies**: Beyond physical defense, women must know how to use behavioral strategies to de-escalate or avoid confrontations.

    - **Insight:** Many training programs fail to cover verbal and non-verbal communication skills, which can help diffuse a potential attack before it escalates into physical violence.

- **Realistic Training Scenarios:** Larkin advocates for realistic training that simulates attack scenarios, helping women build the confidence and experience to respond effectively.

    - **Insight:** Traditional self-defense classes often use controlled environments that do not accurately replicate the stress and unpredictability of real-life attacks.

- **Statistical Reality:** The statistics highlight the pervasive nature of violence against women and the need for a more holistic approach to self-protection.

    - **Insight:** This high rate of assault indicates that many women are not adequately prepared to prevent or defend against attacks, underscoring the need for comprehensive education on personal safety.

By addressing these broader issues, Tim Larkin believes women can be better equipped to defend themselves physically, prevent and respond to threats more effectively, and be empowered.

Understanding Predators: Who, What, Where, Why, and How They Hunt

Who They Are: Predators can come from any background, but often they share certain psychological traits such as narcissism, lack of empathy, and manipulative behavior. They may present themselves as charming or trustworthy to gain the trust of their victims. Predators include serial killers, sexual offenders, stalkers, and abusive partners, friends, or co-workers. Each type has distinct behaviors and methods for selecting and pursuing victims.

What They Do: Predators seek to exert control and dominance over their victims. This can manifest as physical violence, sexual assault, psychological manipulation, or stalking. They often use grooming techniques to build a sense of trust and dependence in their victims before attacking. This may involve flattery, gifts, or isolating the victim from their support network.

Where They Hunt: Predators can operate anywhere, but common hunting grounds include public places like bars and clubs, online platforms, workplaces, and even within the victim's home environment. They may frequent places where potential victims are likely to be alone or vulnerable, such as parking lots, parks, or secluded areas.

Why They Hunt: Predators' motivations can vary but often include a need for power, control, and gratification. Some may have deep-seated psychological issues or a history of abuse themselves. Many predators seek the thrill of the hunt and derive pleasure from the suffering of their victims. For some, the act of predation fulfills a compulsive need.

How They Hunt: Predators typically target and select victims who appear vulnerable, isolated, or easily manipulated. This could be someone physically weaker, emotionally distressed, looking at their phone, or lacking a solid support network. They often use a combination of charm, deceit, and coercion to lure their victims. Once the victim is isolated, the predator may use threats or physical force to maintain control.

Understanding the Mind of an Attacker

In "Survive the Unthinkable: A Total Guide to Women's Self-Protection," Tim Larkin explores the mindset of an attacker to help women better understand how to protect themselves. Here are some key insights, each accompanied by an example:

- **Predatory Nature:** Attackers often have a predatory mindset, seeking easy targets who appear vulnerable or distracted. For example, an attacker might target a woman engrossed in her phone while walking alone at night, perceiving her as less aware of her surroundings.

- **Opportunity and Control**: Attackers look for situations where they can exert control over their victims with minimal risk to themselves. For example, an attacker may wait in a secluded parking garage, knowing it's less likely that someone will intervene or witness the assault.

- **Dehumanization:** Many attackers dehumanize their victims to justify their actions, viewing them as objects rather than individuals with rights and feelings. For example, an attacker might rationalize their behavior by convincing themselves that the victim "deserved it" because of how they dressed or acted.

- **Testing Boundaries:** Attackers often test potential victims' boundaries before fully committing to an attack. For example, an attacker might make inappropriate comments or invade personal space to see if the woman resists or is too intimidated to respond.

- **Psychological Manipulation:** Attackers use psychological tactics to manipulate and intimidate their victims, instilling fear and compliance. For example, an attacker might threaten a woman with harm to her loved ones if she doesn't comply, creating fear and forcing her into submission.

- **Anticipation of Resistance:** While attackers prefer easy targets, they are also prepared for some level of resistance. For example, an attacker might carry a weapon or have a plan for quickly subduing a victim if she tries to fight back, underscoring the importance of being proactive and decisive in self-defence.

By understanding these aspects of an attacker's mindset, women can better recognize potential threats and take proactive steps to protect themselves. Larkin emphasizes the importance of awareness, setting boundaries, and assertiveness in countering attackers' strategies.

Avoidance Recommendations

These books provide numerous lessons and insights into predatory behavior, predator psychology, and methods for prevention and awareness. Here are the critical lessons learned from each book:

Survive the Unthinkable: A Total Guide to Women's Self-Protection" by Tim Larkin is a comprehensive resource dedicated to empowering women with the knowledge and skills necessary to protect themselves. The book emphasizes the importance of understanding your environment, identifying safe places and exits, and learning basic self-defense techniques that target vulnerable points on an attacker's body. Everyday objects can also be used effectively as safety tools.

Inside the Mind of a Predator: This book provides an in-depth look at the psychological, verbal, and physical tactics used by predators to target women. It includes prevention strategies and insights to help women recognize and avoid potentially dangerous situations.

The New Predator: Women Who Kill: Profiles of Female Serial Killers" by Deborah Schurman-Kauflin: Based on face-to-face interviews with female serial killers, this book highlights the psychological profiles and methods used by these women. It provides professionals and the public with valuable information on identifying warning signs and understanding the differences between male and female killers. The book also discusses how these women select their victims and their motivations for killing.

The Human Predator: A Historical Chronicle of Serial Murder and Forensic Investigation by Katherine Ramsland: Traces the history of serial killers and the evolution of forensic investigation. It offers insights into the minds of notorious killers and the methods used to track and capture them. The book provides a comprehensive overview of how predatory behaviors have been understood and investigated throughout history.

All the President's Women: Donald Trump and the Making of a Predator. This book details numerous allegations of sexual misconduct against Donald Trump, providing a broader context of how predatory behavior can manifest in positions of power. It includes interviews and behind-the-scenes reporting that shed light on the tactics and patterns of such predators.

General Lessons Across All Books:

- **Psychological Insights**: Gaining a deeper understanding of the psychological underpinnings of predatory behavior.
- **Behavioral Indicators**: Recognizing early warning signs and behavioral indicators of potential predators.
- Importance of Education: The crucial role of educating the public, especially vulnerable groups, on recognizing and preventing predatory behavior.
- **Support Systems**: Support systems for victims are needed, and providing resources and assistance to those affected by predatory actions is essential.

These books and resources offer valuable insights into predators' mindsets, enabling women to understand and protect themselves from potential dangers. They provide psychological perspectives and practical guidance on recognizing and responding to threats. You can find these books on platforms like Amazon, Goodreads, and various academic publishers.

Seconds Matter

How Awareness, Preparation, and Swift Action Can Save Lives

Understanding the brain's response time in high-stress situations is crucial for implementing adequate safety and self-defense measures. While the brain can process information rapidly, various factors can delay immediate reactions.

The "3-second rule" emphasizes the need for quick assessment, decision-making, and action to ensure safety. Factors like cognitive load, stress responses, decision-making complexities, lack of experience, distractions, and physiological conditions can slow down the brain's response.

We encourage individuals to remain aware, prepared, and decisive, thereby reducing hesitation and enhancing their ability to protect themselves effectively. Being mentally prepared can significantly improve safety outcomes, whether assessing a threat, deciding on the best response, or taking swift action.

Various factors can influence the brain's response time, which can sometimes take up to three seconds. And in high-stress situations, several factors can affect response speed:

Cognitive Load: The brain must process significant information to assess a threat. This includes sensory input, memories, and potential outcomes, which can take time.

Stress Response: High-stress situations can trigger the fight-or-flight response, which sometimes causes a moment of freezing or indecision as the brain determines the best course of action.

Decision-Making: Evaluating options and choosing the best response involves complex neural processes. The brain must weigh the risks and benefits, which can slow down the immediate reaction.

Experience and Training: Individuals trained in self-defense or emergency response often react more quickly because their brains are conditioned to respond rapidly to specific stimuli. Lack of knowledge can lead to longer decision-making times.

- **Distraction and Situational Awareness:** If a person is distracted or unaware of their surroundings, recognizing a threat and responding accordingly can take longer.

- **Physiological Factors**: Fatigue, alcohol, drugs, or medical conditions can impair cognitive and motor functions, slowing response times.

The 3-second rule for safety and self-defense refers to the principle that, during a potentially dangerous or threatening situation, individuals should be able to assess, react, and move to a safer position within three seconds.

This rule emphasizes the importance of making quick decisions and taking immediate action to protect oneself. Here are the critical aspects of the 3-second rule:

- **Assessment**: Quickly evaluate the situation to understand the threat level. Look for potential escape routes, identify any immediate dangers, and decide on the best action.

- **Reaction**: Based on your assessment, decide how to respond. This may include relocating to a safer location, preparing to defend yourself, or employing verbal de-escalation techniques.

- **Action**: Execute your chosen response. This could involve moving away from the threat, using self-defense techniques, or calling for help.

It is essential to be aware of your surroundings and prepared to act swiftly in an emergency. This will reduce hesitation and ensure that individuals can protect themselves effectively in dangerous situations.

Source: The graphic originated from WomenWorking.com, where it was published as part of their personal-safety and empowerment content.

"In the Blink of an Eye: 3 Seconds Can Change Your Life" by Jesse Blackadder offers advice and examples on safety and the importance of making quick decisions. While I can't provide specific excerpts from the book, I can summarize some of the general advice and types of examples that books on this topic typically include:

Advice

- **Stay Aware**: Always be mindful of your surroundings. Situational awareness is crucial in recognizing potential threats early.

- **Trust Your Instincts**: If something feels off, trust your gut feelings. Your intuition is often a valuable guide in dangerous situations.

- **Prepare Mentally and Physically**: Regularly consider potential scenarios and how you would react. Practice self-defense techniques and have a plan in place.

- **React Quickly but Calmly:** Take a moment to assess the situation in a crisis, then act decisively. Remaining calm can help you think more clearly and make better, more informed decisions.

- **Have a Plan:** Know your escape routes, safe places, and have contingency plans in place. Being prepared can make a significant difference in emergencies.

Practical Scenarios

- **Walking Alone at Night:** Advice on how to stay safe by choosing well-lit paths, avoiding distractions like headphones, and being aware of surroundings.

- **Driving:** Tips on defensive driving, including maintaining a safe distance, being vigilant for erratic drivers, and knowing how to respond to sudden hazards.

- **Home Safety**: Securing your home, including installing alarms, utilizing sturdy locks, and developing an emergency plan.

Emergency Responses

- **Fire Safety**: Knowing evacuation routes, having fire extinguishers readily available, and practicing fire drills are essential.

- **Medical Emergencies:** Guidance on quickly assessing and responding to medical emergencies, including CPR and first aid.

This advice and examples illustrate how a few seconds of quick thinking and preparation can significantly ensure safety and prevent harm.

Understanding the brain's response time in high-stress situations is crucial for implementing adequate safety and self-defense measures. Books and resources that delve into this topic provide valuable insights into quick decision-making, situational awareness, and practical self-defense strategies.

Finally, when reviewing "Just 2 Seconds: Using Time and Space to Defeat Assassins and Other Adversaries" by Gavin de Becker, Tom Taylor, and Jeff Marquart is a comprehensive guide on personal protection and threat management.

It emphasizes the critical moments leading up to an attack, highlighting the importance of a swift and immediate reaction to prevent harm. The book includes detailed analyses of numerous attacks, offering practical lessons for protectors and individuals on how to respond to imminent threats effectively. It is a valuable resource for anyone involved in security and threat assessment.
https://just2seconds.org/

Sources:

"The Gift of Fear" by Gavin de Becker focuses on trusting intuition and recognizing warning signs to stay safe.

"In the Blink of an Eye: 3 Seconds" Can Change Your Life. Jesse Blackadder offers advice and examples on making quick decisions and prioritizing safety.

Understanding Self-Defense Laws

Navigate the Differences in Rights to Protect Yourself Effectively

Understanding your right to self-defense is crucial, particularly considering the complexities and variations in the law across different jurisdictions. Generally, self-defense laws allow you to protect yourself from imminent harm, but the specifics, such as the requirement to retreat or the extent of force that can be used, vary significantly by state or province.

Additionally, special considerations come into play in domestic violence situations, where the history of abuse and the ongoing nature of threats are critical factors.

Laws like the Violence Against Women Act (VAWA) provide further protections and support for victims of domestic violence and sexual assault. Knowing these laws and your rights can empower you to act confidently and appropriately in dangerous situations.

You have the right to defend yourself, which is generally recognized under self-defense laws. However, the specifics of this right can vary by jurisdiction.

Section 1: Principles of Self-Defense Law:

- **Reasonable Belief:** You must reasonably believe you are in imminent danger of harm or unlawful force. The threat must be present, immediate, and not based on a future or hypothetical scenario.

- **Proportional Response:** The force used in self-defense must be proportional to the threat. Excessive force beyond what is necessary to prevent harm can not be justified unless violent threats or abduction are occurring at that time.

- **Duty to Retreat (Varies by State):** Some states have a "duty to retreat" requirement, where you must attempt to avoid the confrontation if possible before using force. Other states have "Stand Your Ground" laws, which permit the use of force without retreating if you are lawfully present.

- **Castle Doctrine**: Many states have laws that extend the right to use force, including deadly force, to protect your home (the "castle doctrine"). This principle generally applies when someone unlawfully enters your home and threatens your safety.

- **Defense of Others:** You can use reasonable force to defend others in imminent danger of harm. The same principles of reasonable belief and proportional response apply.

- **No Aggressor:** You cannot claim self-defense if you were the initial aggressor or provoked the confrontation. However, if you withdraw from the confrontation and communicate your intent to stop, and the other party continues to attack, you may regain the right to self-defense.

Example of Legal Text (Hypothetical State Law):

Use of Force in Defense of Person: A person is justified in using force against another when and to the extent that they reasonably believe it is necessary to defend themselves or a third person against the imminent use of unlawful force. A person may use deadly force if they reasonably believe it is required to prevent imminent death, serious bodily injury, kidnapping, or sexual assault.

- **Duty to Retreat**: A person is not required to retreat if they are in a place where they have a legal right to be. This section does not apply if the person using force is engaged in unlawful activity.

- **Defense of Dwelling:** A person is justified in using deadly force to defend their dwelling if they reasonably believe it is necessary to prevent or terminate an unlawful entry or attack. The use of force is presumed to be reasonable if the person against whom the force was used was in the process of unlawfully and forcibly entering or had unlawfully and forcibly entered the dwelling.

While self-defense laws provide the right to protect oneself from harm, the specifics can vary significantly depending on the jurisdiction. It is vital to be familiar with the laws in your area and understand the principles that guide self-defense claims. If you are involved in a self-defense incident, it is advisable to seek legal counsel to navigate the complexities of the law.

Key Differences in Domestic Situations:

- **Context and History:** In domestic violence cases, the history of abuse and the relationship between the parties involved can play a significant role in legal proceedings. Courts may consider patterns of abuse, past incidents, and the ongoing nature of the threat when evaluating self-defense claims.

- **Battered Woman Syndrome:** This is a psychological condition that can affect individuals who have been subjected to prolonged domestic abuse. It may be used in court to help explain why a person in a domestic violence situation believed they were in imminent danger and why their response was reasonable.

- **No Duty to Retreat:** In many jurisdictions, the "duty to retreat" requirement is relaxed or does not apply in one's home, which is often relevant in domestic violence cases. The "Castle Doctrine" typically supports the right to use force, including deadly force, without retreating when in your home.

- **Imminence of Threat:** The concept of imminent threat can be more nuanced in domestic violence cases. Courts may recognize that the threat does not need to be immediate in the same way as in other situations because of the ongoing nature of domestic abuse and the potential for future harm.

- **Protective Orders:** Violation of protective orders by the abuser can be a factor in self-defense claims. If an abuser violates a restraining order, the victim's use of force in response to perceived threats may be more easily justified.

- **Law Enforcement Response:** Police and courts often take domestic violence seriously and may have specialized units and protocols to handle these cases. This can affect the initial response, investigation, and legal proceedings.

- **Documentation:** Keeping records of past abuse, such as photographs, medical records, and police reports, can be crucial in supporting a self-defense claim in a domestic violence situation.

- **Witnesses:** Testimony from friends, family members, neighbors, or others who are aware of the abuse can be valuable in establishing the context of ongoing threats.

- **Seeking Help:** Victims of domestic violence are encouraged to seek help from shelters, support groups, and legal advocates. These resources can provide immediate safety and long-term support.

- **Legal Representation:** It's essential to have legal representation experienced in domestic violence cases. They can navigate the complexities of the law and ensure that the victim's rights and experiences are represented adequately in court.

Understanding the legal principles of self-defense is crucial, whether you are defending yourself or another person. Both scenarios require a reasonable belief in imminent danger and a proportional response to the threat. However, defending another person, especially a child, often invokes additional considerations due to vulnerability.

Jurisdictions vary on the duty to retreat, with some requiring it and others allowing the use of force without retreating if lawfully present. Familiarizing yourself with these laws ensures you can act appropriately in dangerous situations while remaining within legal boundaries.

Defending Another Person:

When defending another person, you must reasonably believe they are in imminent danger of harm or unlawful force. The threat must be immediate and not based on a hypothetical scenario. The force used to defend another must be proportional to the threat, meaning excessive force is unjustified. Some jurisdictions require an attempt to retreat before using force, while others do not. Special considerations apply when defending children, as they are more vulnerable and often warrant a higher duty of care.

- **Reasonable Belief:** You must reasonably believe that the person you defend is in imminent danger of harm or unlawful force. The threat must be immediate and not based on a future or hypothetical scenario.

- **Proportional Response:** The force used to defend another person must be proportional to the threat. Excessive force beyond what is necessary to prevent harm is generally not justified.

- **Duty to Retreat (Varies by Jurisdiction):** Some states require you to attempt to avoid the confrontation, if possible, before using force. In contrast, others allow you to use force without retreating if you are lawfully present.

- **Special Considerations for Children:** Defending a child often invokes a higher duty of care and may be more readily justified due to the child's vulnerability.

- **Defending Yourself:** In self-defence, you must reasonably believe you are in imminent danger of harm. The force must be proportional to the threat faced, avoiding excessive force. Jurisdictions vary on the duty to retreat, with some requiring it and others allowing you to stand your ground if lawfully present. The Castle Doctrine, applicable in many states, permits the use of force, including deadly force, to protect your home from unlawful entry and threats to your safety.

- **Proportional Response: Reasonable Belief:** You must reasonably believe you are in imminent danger of harm or unlawful force. The force used in self-defense must be proportional to the threat faced. Excessive force beyond what is necessary to prevent damage is not justified.

- **Duty to Retreat (Varies by Jurisdiction):** Like defending others, some states require a "duty to retreat," whereas others have "Stand Your Ground" laws that permit the use of force without retreating if you are lawfully present.

Examples of State Differences

- **California:** Has the Castle Doctrine and allows for consideration of BWS in self-defense claims. California law emphasizes the reasonableness of the belief that force was necessary.

- **Florida**: A prominent Stand Your Ground state, which means individuals do not have a duty to retreat anywhere they have a legal right to be.

- **New York:** Requires a duty to retreat if safely possible before using deadly force in self-defence, except in one's home.

Self-defense laws and their application in domestic violence situations can vary widely depending on the state or province.

Understanding the specific legal framework in your jurisdiction is essential. Individuals facing such situations should seek legal counsel to navigate these complex laws and protect their rights.

Home Safety Tips

Strategies for Staying Safe at Home

Ensuring personal safety is paramount for women today, whether at home, in public, or online. By adopting proactive strategies, women can significantly reduce their risk of encountering dangerous situations and enhance their overall sense of security.

This guide offers practical advice on maintaining situational awareness, securing one's home safely, and utilizing technology effectively. Empower yourself with these essential safety measures to stay protected and confident in all aspects of life.

Here are the top measures women can take to secure their homes. The following chapters will expand on each topic:

1. **Strengthen Doors and Windows**

    - **Reinforce Entry Doors:** Use solid-core or metal doors with heavy-duty deadbolts and strike plates. Consider installing a peephole or a video doorbell.

- **Install Window Locks**: Secure windows with locks or add window security film to make the glass more shatter resistant.
- **Use Door and Window Alarms:** These can alert you and your security system if someone tries to open them.

2. Improve Outdoor Lighting

- Use Motion-Sensor Lights: Place these around entry points, pathways, and dark corners to illuminate suspicious activity.
- Install Timed Lights: Use a timer or bright lights to make it appear like someone is home, even when you're not.

3. Establish Safe Habits

- **Keep Doors and Windows Locked**: Always lock doors and windows, even when you are at home.
- **Don't Open the Door to Strangers:** Use a peephole or video doorbell to see who is outside before opening the door.
- **Secure Spare Keys:** Avoid hiding spare keys outside. Instead, consider giving them to a trusted neighbor or using a smart lock with access codes.

4. Maintain Landscaping
- **Trim Shrubs and Trees:** Keep bushes and trees around your home trimmed to eliminate potential hiding spots for intruders.
- **Use Thorny Plants:** Plant thorny bushes near windows and fences to deter burglars.

5. Garage Security
- **Secure Garage Doors:** Use a firm lock on garage doors and never leave them open or unattended.
- **Disable Remote Openers:** If you're going on vacation, consider disabling the garage door opener to prevent unauthorized access.

6. Secure Valuables
- **Use a Safe:** Store valuable items such as jewelry, important documents, and cash in a secure, hidden safe.
- Hide Small Valuables: Don't leave small items of value, like electronics or personal documents, visible from the outside.

7. Install a Security System
- **Choose a Comprehensive Security System**: Systems that include cameras, motion detectors, door/window sensors, and alarms. Modern systems also allow remote monitoring through smartphones.

- **Display Security Signs:** Even if you don't have a system installed, placing security signs and stickers can deter intruders.

8. Smart Home Devices
- **Video Doorbells** allow you to see, hear, and speak remotely to anyone at your door.
- **Smart Locks:** These can be controlled remotely and provide temporary access to guests or service workers without needing a physical key.

9. Emergency Plans
- **Create an Emergency Plan:** Establish an emergency plan (e.g., break-ins, fire). Practice these plans regularly.
- **Keep Emergency Numbers Handy:** Ensure you have quick access to emergency contacts and numbers.

10. Community Awareness
- **Join or Start a Neighborhood Watch:** Participating in a community network can increase security and awareness.
- **Communicate with Neighbors:** Let your trusted neighbors know if you will be away and ask them to monitor your property.

Implementing these measures can significantly enhance home security and provide peace of mind against unwanted predators.

Still, it will not help if the person you are afraid of lives with you. If you exhibit any of the signs below in your relationship, consider seeking help and advice to safely escape your situation.

Signs of Domestic Abuse

- Controlling, hiding, or refusing access to money
- Refusing access to reliable, safe, at-will transportation
- Denying you access to all financial records
- Refusing to put your name on ownership documents of shared property
- Denying you access to bank accounts or credit cards
- Forging your signature, or removing your name from accounts without your permission or knowledge
- Opening your private mail

October is Domestic Violence Awareness Month.

10 Secrets Burglars Do Not Want You to Know

Insider Tips to Protect Your Home and Keep Intruders at Bay

Source: User-generated Internet Meme, circulated widely on social media and email.

Here are ten things a burglar will likely not tell you:

1. **I look for weaknesses in your security."**
   - Weak locks, poor lighting, no security cameras, and a lack of alarms are all signs that a home might be an easy mark. A well-lit, secure, monitored property is less likely to be targeted.

2. **"Your daily routine is valuable intel."**
   - Burglars often watch houses to learn when you're not home. They know the patterns of your comings and goings, so they prefer to strike when you're away.

3. **"I love easy entry points."**
   - Unlocked doors and windows, garage doors left open, or hidden spare keys are the easiest ways for burglars to gain entry. Many will check these before attempting a break-in.

4. **"Yard maintenance tells me if you're home."**
   - An overgrown lawn, uncollected mail, or packages left at the door signal that no one is home, making it a prime target.

5. **"I avoid homes with security signs."**
   - Even a simple sign or sticker from a security company, whether you have a system or not, can deter a burglar who doesn't want to risk triggering an alarm or being caught on camera.

6. **"I knock on doors first."**
   - Burglars often knock or ring the doorbell to see if anyone is home. If someone answers, they might pretend to be lost, selling something, or looking for a friend.

7. **"Valuables are usually in the master bedroom."**
   - The master bedroom is a shared place for a burglar to check first for valuables like jewelry, cash, and electronics. Safes, like a child's room, should be well-hidden or in unexpected places.

8. **"Dogs can be a problem."**
   - Most burglars avoid homes with barking dogs, significantly larger breeds. A noisy dog can draw unwanted attention to their activities. Put up signs.

9. **"I don't want to spend too much time inside."**
   - Burglars aim for quick in-and-out jobs, usually within 10 minutes. Anything that slows them down or risks discovery, such as complex locks or security systems, can prompt them to move on.

10. **"Social media is my reconnaissance tool."**
    - Posting about your vacation plans, expensive new purchases, or even your absence from home can be a goldmine for burglars looking for easy targets.

Knowing these insights can help protect your home and deter potential burglars.

Secure Your Home, Apartment, or Hotel Room

Doors, Stairs, Windows, and Locks

Reinforce Doors:
- Use solid-core or metal doors with heavy-duty deadbolts and strike plates.
- If there is a window on the door, it can be smashed.
- Consider installing a peephole or a video doorbell. Do not open the door unless you know who is there. Verify with ID.
- Put a lock on each door inside to lock yourself into each room.
- Keep windows and doors closed and always locked at night and when you are gone.
- If you want to be alerted if a door is opened, put a shopkeeper's bell or alarm on it.

Cover Windows:
- Check shades and drapes to see if you can see through them. If you can, replace them with dark, thick ones.
- Window Screens and screen doors can be cut. If you need them open, consider installing a metal frame to prevent unauthorized entry.
- **Secure Sliding Doors and Windows:** For added protection, use security bars or rods and consider window locks or security film.
- **Avoid Leaving Windows Open When Unattended:** Open windows can be risky even on higher floors.

Multi-Floor Buildings and Apartments

Entryway Security
- **Install a Peephole or Video Doorbell:** This lets you see who's at your door without opening it.
- **Use Deadbolts and Reinforced Doors:** Ensure your front door is solid and equipped with a deadbolt.
- **Avoid Buzzing in Strangers:** Never allow someone you don't know to enter the building, even if they claim to deliver a package or service.

Common Areas
- **Be Aware of Your Surroundings:** Always pay attention when using elevators, stairwells, or parking garages.
- **Report Unusual Activity:** Notify building management of suspicious behavior or maintenance issues that could compromise security.

Building Entrances and Exits
- **Use Well-Lit Entrances:** Avoid poorly lit or isolated entrances, especially at night.
- **Know Emergency Exits:** Familiarize yourself with all exits and ensure they are accessible.
- **Elevators:** Stand close to the buttons to control the situation.

- **Conference Rooms:** Know your exits, and now, because of shooters, put bodies between you and the doors.

Lodging Safety Tips

Selecting secure and accessible lodging is crucial, especially when traveling solo. Here are some guidelines to help ensure your safety and comfort:

Before You Travel

- **Research Accommodations Thoroughly:** Look for reviews that address safety concerns. Platforms like TripAdvisor and Google Reviews can provide insights into past guest experiences.

- **Book Your First Night in Advance:** Secure your initial lodging before departure, and if possible, arrange your entire stay. You are more vulnerable when you first arrive in an unfamiliar location.

- **Plan Backup Options:** Consider alternative accommodations if your initial choice is not as expected.

Location Considerations

- **Proximity to Transportation and Services:** For convenience and safety, choose lodging near public transportation, hospitals, and other essential services.

- **Crime Rate Awareness:** Research the safety of the area where your lodging is located. Ask the front desk about areas to avoid walking or going due to safety issues. See the end of the Chapter.

- **Accessibility Needs:** If you require specific accommodations such as elevators or ramps, confirm their availability with the hotel before booking.

- **Ask where your room is located**
    - Try to be near an elevator or lobby, not in a remote area near the stairs
    - Do not yell your room# to your friends. Text it. There are people in the lobby watching and listening.

- **Optimal Floor Choice:** Choose a room between the third and sixth floors, less accessible to intruders but still reachable by emergency services.

- **Proximity to Exits:** Familiarize yourself with the emergency exits and evacuation routes in an emergency.

Safety Features

- **24-Hour Reception:** Opt for hotels with a 24-hour front desk. Report any suspicious activity to the staff immediately.

- **Security Measures:** Consider hotels with security features like gated access or on-site security personnel.

- **Key Safety:** Keep your room key separate from the Key packet to prevent revealing your room number.

- **Make sure you are not followed to your room:** If you are uncomfortable, turn around and go back to the lobby and get security.

In Your Room

- **Inspect the Room:** Check behind curtains, under the bed, and in closets to ensure the room is secure.

- **Functionality Check:** Test the phone, locks on windows and doors, and the condition of smoke detectors and fire extinguishers.

- **Privacy Measures:** Verify that curtains close properly and offer privacy.

- **Check for Unusual Electronics:** Be cautious of suspicious devices indicating hidden cameras and report any concerns to hotel management.

- o **If someone knocks on the door, check the peephole; Do Not say anything. If not invited, call security.**

- **Make sure the phone works in the room:** Because sometimes Cell phones do not.

By following these guidelines, you can make informed decisions and enhance your safety while traveling. Always prioritize your well-being and choose accommodations that meet your safety and accessibility needs.

General Safety Tips
- **Lock Your Doors and Windows:** Always lock up, even if you're going to the laundry room or checking the mail.
- **Get to Know Your Neighbors:** Building rapport with your neighbors can create a safer environment and help you recognize unfamiliar faces.
- **Secure Valuables:** Keep personal documents and valuables in a safe and avoid leaving them in easily accessible locations.
- **Be Cautious with social media:** Avoid posting your location or vacation plans publicly.
- **Keys:** Leave one with a neighbor, give a description to the police when you are out of town, and put car keys in the bedroom at night.

These tips can help enhance your safety and security in an apartment or multi-floor building.

True story: The case from Winchendon, Massachusetts, featured on "America's Most Wanted" involved Wayne W. Chapman, a convicted sex offender. Chapman, who had a history of child molestation and rape, entered my friend's house through the 2nd-floor window as he cut the screen next to the stairs.

His escape and evasion of authorities made him a fugitive, and "America's Most Wanted" featured his case to help locate him. Chapman was eventually recaptured and served time for his crimes. I consulted with her on securing her home and regaining a sense of safety in society. It turned out she was his kindergarten teacher.

Data is Key to Safety

These resources offer a comprehensive range of crime statistics and analysis for various regions and periods, providing valuable insights for research or general knowledge.

Here are some free websites where you can find crime rate statistics:

- **FBI Crime Data Explorer:** The FBI provides comprehensive crime data for the United States, including violent crime, property crime, and arrest statistics. You can explore crime trends and view data by state, city, or county. FBI Crime Data Explorer

- **Bureau of Justice Statistics (BJS):** The BJS offers detailed crime statistics, including national surveys on crime victimization, law enforcement data, and corrections statistics. Bureau of Justice Statistics

- **NeighborhoodScout:** This site provides crime data by city or neighborhood in the United States. It includes crime maps, school ratings, and real estate trends. It offers some free information, but detailed reports may require a subscription. NeighborhoodScout

- **City-Data:** City-Data offers crime statistics, housing data, and other demographic information for U.S. cities. You can explore and compare crime rates in different neighborhoods. City-Data Crime Rates

- **Statista:** Although Statista is primarily a paid resource, it offers various free statistics, including crime rates, trends, and comparisons between countries and regions. Statista - Crime Statistics

On Road Safety

Essential Vehicle Security Strategies and Habits

The dangers of sharing too much personal information via bumper stickers and window decals

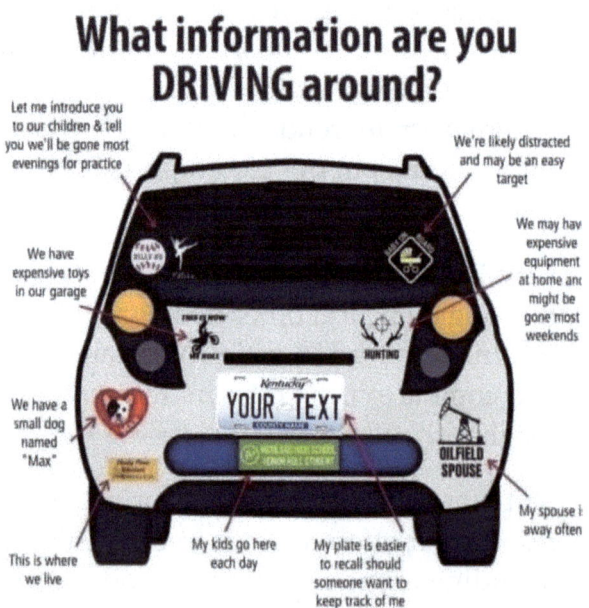

Source: What Info are you driving around? The Sheriff's Department warns of bumper stickers and decals. Fox 11 Los Angeles, Mary Stringin, Feb 9, 2021, Crime and Public Safety

Whether running errands, commuting, or traveling alone, adopting smart habits around your car can dramatically improve your safety.

Follow these common-sense strategies every time you get behind the wheel:

Plan Your Route
- **Know Your Route:**
    - Ahead of time, by using a GPS with real-time updates and being familiar with alternative routes in case of road closures or detours.
- **Stick to well-traveled roads**
    - Favor busy, well-lit streets over shortcuts through isolated neighborhoods.

Approaching Your Vehicle

- **Keys in hand.** Grip your key fob before you leave the building to unlock and enter quickly.

- **Stay alert.** Don't talk on your phone or text while you walk. Keep your head up and scan your surroundings.

- **Inspect the area.** Look around and under your car for anyone loitering or hiding. If something feels off, retreat to safety, call 911, or trigger your car alarm.

Locking & Securing Your Car

- **One-click entry.** Program your remote so a single press unlocks the driver's door; a second press unlocks the rest.

- **Lock instantly.** Hit "lock" as soon as you're inside—never wait until you're driving off.

- **Windows up.** Keep windows rolled up (or only partially down) when stopped in traffic or at a traffic light.

Settling In

- **Pause before you go.** Don't lower your windows or open a sunroof until you're confidently on the move.

- **Stow valuables.** Tuck purses, phones, and other items out of sight—ideally in your trunk.

Parking Safety

- **Choose wisely.** Park in well-lit, populated areas. Avoid spots beside large vehicles or in dark corners.

- **Have your key ready.** Approach your car with your fob in hand to unlock and enter without fumbling.

Staying Focused on the Road

- **Minimize distractions.** Keep calls and texts to a minimum. If you must use your phone, pull safely to the side.

- **Trust your gut.** If you feel uneasy, leave the area or call for help, whether parked or driving.

Dealing with Strangers

- **Don't stop for unsolicited help.** If someone flags you down, drive to the nearest public, well-lit place (such as a gas station, police station, or hospital).

- **If you're being followed:** Alert a friend, remain in motion, and head straight to a safe, crowded location.

Emergency Preparedness

- **Build a car kit.** Keep essentials like a first-aid kit, flashlight, blanket, water, snacks, and a phone charger onboard.

- **Know your vehicle.** Maintain regular service, check fluids and tire pressure, and carry tools (e.g., air pump, jack, fix-a-flat).

- **Breakdown protocol:** Stay inside with doors locked, engage hazard lights, and call roadside assistance or 911 if you feel unsafe.

Key Management

- **Hide spare keys wisely.** Never leave extra keys under mats or flowerpots — give them to a trusted friend instead.

- **Keep fobs secure.** When parked, don't let your keys dangle visibly in the ignition or cupholder.

Share Your Whereabouts

- **Location sharing.** Use apps like "Find My" or send a quick location update to a trusted contact whenever you travel alone.

Personal Defense Tools

- **Accessible deterrents.** Carry a wasp spray, pepper spray, or bear spray, walking sticks, a dog leash, a personal alarm, or a tactical flashlight, and quickly deploy them.

- **Strategic placement.** Keep these items in your bag, glove compartment, or center console, where you can easily access them.

Dress for Safety

- **Freedom of movement.** Wear comfortable, non-restrictive clothing and shoes that allow you to move easily.

- **Low profile.** Avoid flashy jewelry or designer bags that might attract unwanted attention.

Traveling is not the Time to Let Your Guard Down

Navigate Cars, Taxis, Planes, and Trains

Traveling to work or going on vacation is not the time to let your guard down. Ensure someone you know understands your schedule. Don't tell strangers what you are up to and avoid sharing rides and dinner with people you have just met.

Tips for Women Travelers

Women traveling abroad may encounter unique health and security risks. Here are some essential tips to help you prepare and stay safe:

Research Your Destination and Local Customs

Customs and norms vary significantly around the world. Some countries may have specific regulations for behavior, speech, and women's attire. For example, tight-fitting clothing, sleeveless tops, or shorts might not be acceptable in certain cultures. It's crucial to research local customs and laws before you go to ensure your clothing and behavior align with local expectations.

Women's Health Considerations Abroad

Healthcare systems vary from country to country, and some essential items may be difficult to obtain. Packing necessary health items such as feminine hygiene products and birth control is wise, as these may not be readily available where you're going.

Be aware that some countries have strict laws affecting women's health, including restrictions on reproductive health services. In certain places, being pregnant outside of marriage could result in legal consequences, even for victims of sexual assault.

If you're pregnant and planning to travel, check airline policies, as they may restrict travel later in pregnancy. It's advisable to have a note from your healthcare provider confirming it is safe to fly and to ensure your travel insurance covers pregnancy-related costs.

For more detailed information on healthcare abroad, visit the [Your Health Abroad page](#).

Taxi & Rideshare Safety Tips

Rideshare and taxi apps have revolutionized travel — yet stepping into a stranger's car still carries risks. By taking simple precautions before, during, and after your ride, you can significantly reduce those risks and ride with confidence. Below is an expanded set of best practices to keep you safe whenever you hail a cab or tap your favorite rideshare app.

Verify Your Driver
- **Match the Details**
  Before you open the door, confirm that the driver's face, vehicle make/model, and license plate number exactly match what the app displays.
- **Trustworthy Checkpoints**
  If anything doesn't line up or the vehicle arrives early, contact the app's support line rather than stepping into an unknown car.

Sit in the Back Seat
- **Optimal Positioning**
  Ride in the back, ideally behind the front passenger seat. This gives you more space to exit quickly and preserves a respectful distance from the driver.
- **Visibility Advantage**
  You can see the driver's behavior and the road ahead from the rear seat.

Share Your Trip Details
- **Live Location Sharing**
  Use the app's built-in "Share My Ride" feature to broadcast your route and expected arrival to a trusted friend or family member.
- **Check-In Messages**
  Send a quick "I'm on my way" and "I've arrived" text — small actions that create big safety nets.

Monitor the Route
- **Keep the Map On**
  Keep your phone out and the route visible. If the driver takes unexpected detours, ask for clarification immediately.
- **Know Your Exit Points**
  If you ever feel unsafe mid-ride, request to be let out in a well-lit, populated area like a gas station or 24-hour store.

Maintain Professional Boundaries
- **Limit Personal Detail**
  Avoid sharing your home address, travel itinerary, or sensitive information. Stick to neutral topics—favorite music, local landmarks, or the weather.
- **Read the Cues**
  If the driver's conversation turns too personal or makes you uncomfortable, redirect the discussion or fall silent.

Use Emergency Features
- **Familiarize Yourself**
  Spend a few moments locating the "Emergency Assistance" button or equivalent in your app settings.
- **Automatic Alerts**
  In many apps, activating this feature will alert local authorities and send your exact coordinates—use it without hesitation if you ever feel threatened.

Exit Safely
- **Scan Before You Step Out**
  Before opening the door, look for oncoming traffic, cyclists, or other hazards.
- **Request a Safe Drop-Off**
  If your destination is poorly lit, ask the driver to pull into a nearby well-populated area before letting you out.

Keep Keys and Essentials Handy
- **"Ready" Mode**
  Have your house or car keys in hand as you exit—fumbling for them in the dark can delay you and draw unwanted attention.
- **Easy Access Tools**
  Store your phone, wallet, and self-defense items in outer pockets or a readily accessible compartment.

Carry Personal Defense Items
- **Pepper Spray or Personal Alarm**
  A small canister of pepper or insect spray, or a loud personal alarm, can deter an attacker and draw attention to your situation.
- **Tactical Key**
  Keep one key on your knuckles or a purpose-built tactical key—easy to grip and ready for use if you need to trigger your car alarm or defend yourself.

Dress for Agility

- **Freedom of Movement**
  Choose shoes and clothing that allow you to run, turn, and defend yourself if needed. Avoid overly restrictive garments.
- **Low-Profile Accessories**
  Leave flashy jewelry and expensive bags at home — they can make you a target and weigh you down.

No single tip guarantees perfect safety, but combining these practices creates layers of protection, making it far more likely you'll arrive at your destination unharmed.

Trust your instincts, stay vigilant, and don't hesitate to use the tools available on your body at your disposal.

With these strategies, you can reclaim rideshare freedom and peace of mind, wherever you're headed.

Secure Journeys: Staying Safe on Trains and Beyond

Practical Strategies for Confident Travel in Public Transit and All Other Modes

Whether boarding a commuter train or exploring a new city on foot, prioritizing personal safety is essential. A few proactive habits—such as choosing populated areas, safeguarding your belongings, and blending in with your surroundings—can significantly reduce your risk and help you travel with confidence.

Train Travel Safety

- **Stay in Populated Cars:**
  Choose a well-lit, busy car—ideally near the conductor or in a women-only section if available. If your vehicle empties out, move to one with more passengers.

- **Secure Your Luggage:**
  Keep bags and valuables within sight or locked. Never leave them unattended, even for a moment.

- **Remain Alert at Stops:**
  Whenever the train pauses, scan for suspicious behavior. If you feel uneasy, switch cars or notify staff immediately.

- **Plan Your Exit:**
  Know your stop in advance. Stand up and gather your belongings a few minutes before arrival so you can disembark smoothly.

- **Ready Your Essentials:**
  Keep keys, tickets, and phone in an easy-to-reach pocket so you won't have to fumble when you step off the bus.

- **Carry Simple Defense Tools:**
  A personal alarm or small door wedge can add security, especially if you're in a sleeper car overnight.

- **Dress for Agility:**
  Wear comfortable clothing with secure pockets. Avoid flashy jewelry that might attract unwanted attention.

General Travel Safety (All Modes)

- **Dress to Blend In:**
  Research local fashion norms and choose neutral, practical clothing. Avoid "tourist" accessories like fanny packs or branded conference badges.

- **Stay Sober and Alert:**
  Limit alcohol or other distractions. Clear-headed awareness is your best defense.

- **Trust Your Instincts:**
  If a situation feels off, remove yourself or seek help — no question is too small regarding your safety.

- **Secure Your Belongings:**
  Use crossbody bags or backpacks worn in front. In cafes and restaurants, tuck valuables under a table or between your feet.

- **Minimize Public Maps & Guidebooks:**
  Glancing repeatedly at a paper map or guidebook marks you as a visitor. Pre-load routes on your phone and use discreet navigation (e.g., one earbud).

- **Limit Oversharing:**
  Travel plans, hotel details, and conference schedules should be kept private, off email (out of office externally), social media, and not said out loud in public conversations.

- **Have Emergency Contacts Ready:**
  Store local authorities, your country's embassy, and a trusted friend's number in your phone and wallet.

- **Learn Basic Self-Defense:**
  A short class can boost your confidence and teach you techniques to buy time until help arrives.

Safe travel combines preparation, awareness, and simple habits—whether on a train platform or exploring downtown streets. You turn everyday routines into powerful layers of protection by choosing crowded cars, safeguarding your valuables, dressing inconspicuously, and trusting your instincts. Empower yourself with these common-sense strategies and enjoy your journeys with peace of mind.

Distraction Crimes

How robbers work

Stay Alert and Be Aware of Your Surroundings:

- Always be conscious of what's happening around you. Be cautious if someone tries to engage you in conversation or commotion. It could be a distraction tactic. Avoid getting too absorbed in your phone or other activities in public places.

Secure Your Belongings:

- Keep your bags close to your body, with zippers and openings facing inward. Use bags that are difficult to open, like anti-theft backpacks with hidden zippers. For briefcases or business bags, consider locks or security cables. Avoid placing valuables in easily accessible pockets, such as jackets or back pockets. When you walk near a street, ensure you are on the Sidewalk, not next to the road, where they can grab you from the street and drive away.

Be Skeptical of Unsolicited Help or Attention:

- Be wary of strangers who offer unsolicited help or engage you with unusual questions, even if they seem harmless or well-meaning. If a group of people approaches you, be cautious of where your belongings are and be ready to move away if you feel uncomfortable.

Avoid Flashing Valuables:

- Do not publicly display expensive electronics, jewelry, or large amounts of cash. If you must use your phone or laptop, do so discreetly and in safe locations. Consider using a nondescript bag for carrying valuables instead of designer bags or cases that signal expensive contents.

Keep Essentials Separate and Secure:

- Divide your valuables. For example, keep credit cards and IDs in different places on your person (e.g., some in a money belt and some in a secure pocket). This way, you don't lose everything, even if one item is stolen. Avoid putting all your valuable items in one bag.

Stay Close to Your Belongings in Public Spaces:

- Never leave your bag or briefcase unattended, even for a moment. If you're in a restaurant or meeting place, keep your bag on your lap or loop the strap around your leg or chair leg. Hold your bag in front of you in crowded areas, such as public transport.

Be Cautious in High-Risk Areas:

- Distraction crimes are more likely in crowded areas like tourist sites, public transportation, or busy restaurants. Keep your back to the wall in these areas and avoid standing or sitting too close to the exit, where thieves can quickly make their getaway.

Practice Safe Travel Habits:

- Plan your routes and know your destinations to minimize the need to ask for directions or look lost. If you need assistance, ask officials or go into a nearby shop instead of asking random passersby. Avoid sharing your travel plans or showing maps in public.

These strategies will help you stay vigilant and protect your belongings from distraction crimes, especially when traveling for business or leisure.

In any threatening situation, your main goal should always be to preserve your safety and that of others. Surrendering your possessions may be difficult, but it is the best choice when faced with potential violence.

It is essential to give a robber what they want instead of resisting or fighting back for several key reasons:

Personal Safety:
- Your safety is the most crucial consideration in a robbery situation. Robbers may be armed or willing to use violence to get what they want. By complying with their demands, you minimize the risk of physical harm to yourself and others around you.

Unpredictable Behavior:
- Robbers can be unpredictable, especially if they are desperate, nervous, or under the influence of substances. Any form of resistance can escalate the situation, potentially leading to violence that could have been avoided.

Valuables Are Replaceable, Life is Not:
- Most material possessions, such as wallets, phones, and jewelry, can be replaced. Your health and life cannot be. It's better to lose belongings than to suffer injuries or worse. Prioritize your well-being over the property.

Minimizing Escalation:
- Attempting to resist or fight back can turn a robbery into a more violent confrontation. Complying with the robber's demands is more likely to end the encounter quickly, without further incident.

Legal and Psychological Ramifications:
- Fighting back can lead to serious legal complications if the robber or bystanders are injured, even if you acted in self-defence. Additionally, the psychological trauma from escalating a dangerous situation can have long-lasting effects.

Robbers Often Just Want to Get Away Quickly:
- Most robbers are looking for a quick and easy opportunity. They typically want to take the valuables and leave without drawing attention or getting caught. Giving them what they wish to reduces the chances of the situation becoming more dangerous.

Preventing Injury to Others:
- If you are in a public place or with others, resisting could put them at risk, too. A robber may react aggressively towards others to regain control if you resist. Complying with the demands helps protect not only yourself but those around you.

Post-Incident Reporting:
- After the situation is resolved safely, you can provide detailed information to law enforcement, including descriptions of the robber, any vehicles involved, and what was taken. This can aid in the investigation and recovery of your belongings.

Compliance

Actions to reduce the risk of further harm

Compliance does not mean agreeing to or condoning the violence; instead, it refers to assessing the situation and taking actions that may help preserve your life and reduce the risk of further harm. It saved my life!

Here are some reasons why compliance might be considered in such extreme situations:

Preservation of Life and Safety:
- The primary goal in any violent situation, including rape, is to survive and minimize physical harm. If you believe resisting could escalate the violence or provoke further aggression, compliance might be a way to reduce immediate risk.

Understanding the Situation:
- Every situation is unique. If the attacker is armed, intoxicated, or displaying unstable behavior, compliance could be the safest option to avoid triggering a more dangerous reaction. Remaining calm and cooperative might de-escalate the aggressor's behavior.

Buying Time:
- Compliance can sometimes provide an opportunity to assess the situation and plan an escape or signal for help. This could involve looking for an opening to run, remembering details about the attacker, or finding a way to alert someone nearby.

Avoiding Further Injury:
- Resistance in some situations might lead to more severe violence, including physical injuries or even death. Complying can be a strategy to prevent further harm if you feel that resisting would provoke a more violent response.

Psychological and Emotional Impact:
- It's essential to remember that compliance does not equal consent. Victims often comply out of fear or a survival instinct. Understanding this can help mitigate feelings of guilt or shame afterward, as the priority is survival

Legal and Medical Follow-up:
- After surviving such an incident, compliance can facilitate providing accurate details to law enforcement and healthcare professionals. This information is crucial for legal proceedings and ensuring proper medical care and psychological support.

Preserving Mental Focus:
- Compliance can sometimes be a way to stay mentally focused and not panic in a highly traumatic situation. Remaining as calm as possible may allow you to think more clearly and potentially take actions that could lead to safety.

Seeking Immediate Help:
- After the immediate threat ends, seek help as quickly as possible. Reporting the crime to authorities, getting medical attention, and contacting support services can help you begin the recovery process and ensure that the perpetrator is held accountable.

Important Considerations:
- **Personal Response Varies:** Every person and situation is different. Some may choose to resist; others may find compliance a better option for survival. There is no "right" or "wrong" way to react to such trauma, and the focus should be on survival and recovery.

- **Seek Support:** If you have experienced such an event, seeking professional support is crucial. Counseling and therapy can help process the trauma and navigate complex emotions.

Ultimately, in situations involving rape or violence, compliance should be understood as a potential strategy for survival and minimizing harm or even death.

Protect Your Financial Accounts

Ensure Your Privacy, Prevent Harassment, and Secure Your Digital Life

← Manitowoc County Sheriff'... 🔍

Manitowoc County Sheriff's Office
1 hr

We normally do not participate in these types of social media posts, but figured it could not hurt this time.

(borrowed this from some other law enforcement agencies)

Where did you grow up: STOP
Favorite color: GIVING
First pet's name: PEOPLE
Street you grew up on: YOUR
Favorite Childs Name: PERSONAL
Favorite sports team: INFO
High school mascot: TO
Favorite food: GUESS
What was your first car: YOUR
Moms name before she married: PASSWORD
First job: AND
Favorite band: SECURITY
Favorite food: QUESTIONS

Source: Manitowoc County Sheriff's Office Facebook Page (Mid 2020

The Internet is an invaluable resource that offers countless opportunities for communication, work, and leisure. However, it also comes with unique challenges and risks, particularly for women.

The digital world can sometimes be daunting, with risks ranging from social media harassment to identity theft and online dating scams. Understanding these risks and adopting proactive safety measures is essential for online privacy, security, and well-being.

Online Financial Safety:

- **Create Strong, Unique Passwords:** For each account, use a mix of letters, numbers, and symbols. Avoid reusing passwords to minimize risk.
- **Enable Two-Factor Authentication (2FA):** Requiring a second verification step adds an extra layer of security.
- **Regularly Monitor Accounts:** Check bank and credit card statements for suspicious activities.
- **Avoid Public Wi-Fi for Financial Transactions:** Use a VPN if accessing sensitive information over public networks.
- **Be Wary of Phishing Scams:** Verify email sources before clicking links or downloading attachments.
- **Log Out After Use:** Always sign out of financial accounts on shared or public devices.

- **Use Verified Banking Apps and Websites:** Access your accounts only through official apps and websites.
- **Keep Software Updated:** Regularly update your devices and apps to protect against security vulnerabilities.

Online Credit Cards vs. Debit Cards

Regarding online transactions, using a credit card is generally safer than using a debit card. Here's why:

Benefits of Using Credit Cards

- **Better Fraud Protection:** Credit cards offer more robust fraud protection. If your card is compromised, you are not liable for unauthorized charges, and the funds do not come directly from your bank account.
- **Dispute Resolution:** Credit card companies provide better support for disputing unauthorized or incorrect charges, making it easier to recover funds.
- **Credit Score Benefits:** Responsible use of credit cards can help build your credit score, unlike debit cards, which don't impact your credit history.
- **Rewards and Cashback:** Many credit cards offer rewards, cashback, or travel points, which can add extra value to your purchases.

Risks of Using Debit Cards
- **Immediate Impact on Funds:** If your debit card is compromised, the money is taken directly from your bank account, which can disrupt your financial plans and take longer to recover.
- **Limited Fraud Protection:** While some banks offer fraud protection for debit cards, it is often less comprehensive than that for credit cards.
- **Lower Dispute Capabilities:** Disputes regarding debit card transactions can be more challenging and time-consuming, and there are fewer protections against unauthorized charges.

Safety Tips for Using Credit and Debit Cards

- **Use Credit Cards for Online Shopping:** I prefer using credit cards for online transactions because they offer enhanced security and dispute options.
- **Enable Alerts:** Set up alerts for all credit and debit card transactions to detect suspicious activity quickly.
- **Limit Debit Card Use:** Reserve your debit card for in-person transactions at trusted locations. Avoid using it for online purchases or at unfamiliar ATMs.

- **Monitor Statements Regularly:** Check credit and debit card statements frequently for unauthorized transactions.
- **Use Virtual Cards:** Some banks and credit card companies offer virtual cards for online purchases. These cards generate a unique card number for each transaction, providing an extra layer of security.

Source: The Security Awareness Company

By understanding the differences and implementing these practices, you can protect your finances more effectively in online transactions.

How to Handle Identity Theft and Credit Card Fraud

If you become a victim of identity theft or credit card fraud, knowing the immediate steps can provide a strong sense of security and preparedness, helping you minimize damage and restore financial protection.

- **Contact Your Card Issuer Immediately:** Call your card issuer's fraud department when you notice any unauthorized activity on your account. They are trained to handle these situations and will help you secure your account, prevent further transactions, and issue a new card if needed.
- **File a Police Report**: Report the incident to your local police department and obtain a copy of the report. This will serve as documentation that you took steps to address the issue and can be helpful when dealing with creditors or filing an Identity Theft Report.

- **Notify the Credit Bureaus**: Place a fraud alert with the three major credit bureaus—Equifax, Experian, and TransUnion. This alert prevents fraudsters from opening new accounts in your name and ensures you will be contacted before any new credit is issued. You only need to contact one bureau; they are legally required to inform the other two within 24 hours.
- **File a Complaint with the FTC:** Report the identity theft to the Federal Trade Commission (FTC). The FTC collaborates with various law enforcement agencies and credit reporting agencies to address identity theft cases. Filing a complaint helps ensure that your case is properly documented and shared with the relevant authorities. File with the CISA Portal: https://myservices.cisa.gov/irf

Acting promptly on these steps is not just about protecting your financial information; it's about being proactive and responsible, and providing relief by initiating the recovery process.

To stay safe on social media, users should thoroughly research digital content before accepting, clicking on, or sharing it.

Everyone receives friend and follower requests, but users should be careful who they accept. For example, if strangers add you, they could attempt to scam you, and others might be bots. If a user can trust the people on their friends list, it is one less thing to worry about.

- **Be Selective with Friend Requests:** Only accept friend or follow requests from people you know. Scammers often use fake profiles to gain access to your personal information.

What should users stay away from?
  o Accounts with no information
  o Accounts with only a few friends
  o Accounts that immediately start sending you messages with no real purpose, especially in broken English
  o Accounts that start sending you links, promising things, asking for investment, or promising love.

- **Adjust Privacy Settings:** Most social media platforms, like Instagram, X, and others, limit who can see your posts, contact you and view your profile information.

- **Avoid Sharing Personal Information:** Don't post sensitive details like your address, phone number, or financial information. Be cautious about sharing your location.

Social media scams and phishing are among the most prevalent issues on social media platforms today. The links for these attacks usually attempt to steal your identity, money, or work to spread a bot or virus to your colleagues, friends, and family network.

- **Beware of Phishing and Scams:** Scammers can use social media to trick you into revealing personal information or clicking on malicious links. Scams and phishing tactics include:
    - Chain letters
    - Quick requests for money, sometimes from friends who have just added you to a new account
    - Links to quizzes and games that require your phone number or bank details first
    - Links to photos and clickbait article titles that take you off the network (likely phishing scams)
    - Shortened URLs, which can be used to hide malware and viruses on a link
    - Pay an upfront fee to work from home/make money
    - Sweepstakes and lottery winnings (these are never distributed through social media, even if you play)
    - Sudden romantic interests asking for money

Some of these social media scams are harmless, but others can be used to actively steal information and money. It's essential to double-check anything before you click on it, and be careful when and how users give information to a third-party site.

This means paying attention to what's being sent and shared, evaluating sources, and investigating anything that seems off or slightly suspicious.

- **Think Before You Share:** Be mindful of what you post; even deleted content can be recovered, or screenshots can be taken.
- **Watch for Impersonation Accounts:** Report fake accounts pretending to be you or someone you know.
- **Be Careful with Apps and Quizzes:** Avoid granting access to your profile or data to third-party apps or quizzes that may misuse your information.

Cyberbullying is Not a Problem Just for Children

41% of Americans have experienced online harassment

In the United States, both women and men experience cyberbullying, but the nature and extent of the harassment vary significantly by gender. Approximately 41% of Americans report having experienced some form of online harassment.

Among those, the most severe forms of harassment, such as physical threats or sexual harassment, have increased from 15% in 2014 to 25% in recent years.

Women vs. Men:

- **Women** are more likely to experience sexual harassment and stalking online. About 16% of women report being sexually harassed online, compared to 5% of men. Similarly, 13% of women have been stalked online, compared to 9% of men.

- **Men** are more likely to report experiencing offensive name-calling and physical threats. Approximately 35% of men have been called offensive names online, compared to 26% of women. Men are also more likely to be physically threatened online, with 16% reporting such incidents versus 11% of women.

Age and Demographic Differences:

- Younger adults, especially those under 30, are particularly prone to online harassment, with nearly 64% reporting some form of harassment. Among this group, women under 35 are more likely to experience severe harassment, with 33% reporting incidents of sexual harassment.

- Black and Hispanic teens report higher rates of cyberbullying related to their race or ethnicity compared to White teens. For example, 21% of Black teens say they have been targeted because of their race, compared to 11% of Hispanic teens and only 4% of White teens.

Overall, while men may face more frequent offensive name-calling and physical threats, women get more severe and targeted forms of online abuse, including sexual harassment and stalking. Addressing these differences is crucial for creating safer online spaces for all users.

If a cyberbully is targeting you, there are steps you can and should take to protect yourself:

- **Do not engage**: The bully is often looking for a reaction. By refusing to respond, you deprive them of the satisfaction they seek. Over time, they may lose interest and move on.

- **Document Everything**: Keep a detailed record of every message, post, or interaction—a comment, email, text, or tweet. Cyberbullies often assume anonymity, but thorough documentation can help build a persuasive case if the situation escalates.

- **Report the Abuse**: Most websites and social platforms have mechanisms for reporting abusive behaviour. If the bully is a colleague, speak with your manager or the HR department. It is crucial for severe cases involving law enforcement, as they are equipped to manage and prosecute online harassment.

- **Block the Bully**: If the bully contacts you through a single platform, blocking them can be an immediate solution. This simple action can cut off their access and prevent further harassment.

- **Seek Support**: Cyberbullying can be isolating and stressful. Reach out to trusted friends or family members. Their support can provide comfort and new perspectives on managing the situation.

- **Consider Changing Contact Information**: Although it's not an ideal solution, changing your email address or phone number may be necessary as a last resort to avoid persistent harassment.

Cyberbullying is a severe issue that can cause significant harm, but by taking initiative and taking steps, you can regain control and protect yourself.

Online Dating Can Be a Positive Experience

Be Aware of the Risks, Take advantage of the Safety Features

Women vs. Men:

- **Women** are more likely to experience sexual harassment and stalking online. About 16% of women report being sexually harassed online, compared to 5% of men. Similarly, 13% of women have been stalked online, compared to 9% of men.

- **Men** are more likely to report experiencing offensive name-calling and physical threats. Approximately 35% of men have been called offensive names online, compared to 26% of women. Men are also more likely to be physically threatened online, with 16% reporting such incidents versus 11% of women.

Age and Demographic Differences:

- Younger adults, especially those under 30, are particularly prone to online harassment, with nearly 64% reporting some form of harassment. Among this group, women under 35 are more likely to experience severe harassment, with 33% reporting incidents of sexual harassment.

- Black and Hispanic teens report higher rates of cyberbullying related to their race or ethnicity compared to White teens. For example, 21% of Black teens say they have been targeted because of their race, compared to 11% of Hispanic teens and only 4% of White teens.

Overall, while men may face more frequent offensive name-calling and physical threats, women experience more severe and targeted forms of online abuse, including sexual harassment and stalking. Addressing these differences is crucial for creating safer online spaces for all users.

Online Dating Risks for Senior Women vs. Women Under 50

Senior Women

- **Scams and Fraud:** Seniors are more likely to be targeted by romance scams, where perpetrators feign romantic interest to solicit money or personal information. About 45% of older online daters report encountering at least one type of scam. This is especially prevalent among those aged 50 to 64 compared to those 65 and older.

- **Unwanted Behavior:** Around one-third of older women on dating platforms have been sent unsolicited explicit content, experienced persistent unwanted contact, or been called offensive names. These behaviors can lead to emotional distress and distrust in using these platforms.

- **Negative Experiences:** Older women are more likely than their male counterparts to report negative experiences with online dating. This group is also less familiar with digital technology, which may increase their vulnerability to manipulation or scams.

Women Under 50

- **Harassment and Threats:** Younger women, particularly those under 30, frequently report receiving unsolicited explicit messages and experiencing harassment. Nearly half of women under 50 have faced unwanted sexual messages or continuous contact after indicating disinterest. This demographic also reports higher levels of anxiety and depression linked to the pressures and negative interactions on swipe-based dating apps like Tinder and Bumble.

- **Scams and Fake Profiles:** Although younger women also face scams, they are generally less frequent than men of the same age group. The prevalence of fake profiles and bots on platforms like Tinder is a significant concern, making it essential for users to verify profiles and avoid sharing personal information too soon.

Key Takeaways

- **Scams:** Senior women are more likely to be targeted by scammers looking for financial gain, whereas younger women face a higher incidence of harassment and unsolicited sexual content.

- **Emotional Impact:** Online dating can cause significant emotional distress for both groups, but younger women are more affected by anxiety and depression related to dating app usage.

- **Preventive Measures:** All users, regardless of features or age, should be cautious about sharing personal information, use platforms with robust security features, and report any suspicious or harmful behavior.

These insights can help tailor strategies for safer online dating experiences, taking into account age-related risks.

Online Dating Safety Tips

- **Use Reputable Dating Sites/Apps:** Choose well-known, reputable platforms with substantial safety and privacy measures.
- **Keep Personal Information Private:** Avoid sharing personal details like your last name, workplace, or address early on.
- **Verify Their Identity:** Before meeting in person, try to verify the person's identity through video calls or social media.
- **Meet in Public Places:** For the first few dates, meet in a public location and arrange your transportation.

- **Inform a Friend or Family Member:** Let someone know where you're going and who you're meeting.
- **Trust Your Instincts:** Don't hesitate to end the conversation or date if something feels off or you're uncomfortable.
- **Be Aware of Scams:** Be wary of people who quickly express strong emotions, ask for money, or share elaborate stories of hardship.
- **Limit Online Communication:** Move conversations off the app when you feel comfortable and avoid sharing your phone number or other contact details too soon.

These tips can help you stay secure while navigating the online world, whether managing finances, engaging on social media, or meeting new people.

Safety of Online Dating Sites: What Customers Say – The Good, The Bad, and The Ugly

The Good:

- **Convenience and Access:** Online dating offers a convenient way to connect with a wide range of people, increasing the chances of finding a compatible match. Apps like Match.com and eHarmony utilize detailed questionnaires to help users find partners who share their values and interests. Platforms such as Hinge and Coffee Meets Bagel focus on quality over quantity, offering daily match suggestions based on compatibility rather than endless swiping

- **Success Stories:** Many users have found meaningful relationships through online dating, which should inspire hope.

- About 12% of U.S. adults have married or entered a committed relationship with someone they met online. Platforms like eHarmony and Match are primarily known for facilitating long-term relationships, focusing on compatibility and serious dating.

- **Safety Features:** Reputable dating sites are committed to your safety, with measures like profile verification, photo moderation, and the ability to report or block suspicious users. For example, Bumble and Hinge offer in-app video chats. This feature allows you to verify identities before meeting in person, providing security and peace of mind.

The Bad:

- **Fake Profiles and Scams:** Despite safety measures, fake profiles and scams are common issues. Users of sites like OkCupid and Zoosk have reported encountering fraudulent accounts and scams. Scammers may attempt to solicit money or personal information, and although platforms work to filter these out, some still manage to get through.

- **Harassment and Unwanted Messages:** Women, in particular, report experiencing harassment and unwanted messages. Platforms like Tinder and Bumble have taken steps to combat this by allowing users to block or report abusers, but the issue remains a significant concern across many dating apps.

- **Ghosting and Miscommunication:** Many users express frustration with "ghosting" — when someone suddenly stops responding — and miscommunication. This is a common complaint across platforms like Tinder and Hinge, where casual interactions can sometimes lead to disappointment when expectations are not met.

The Ugly:

- **Catfishing and Identity Theft:** Catfishing, where someone pretends to be someone else online, is a severe issue on dating platforms like Plenty of Fish and Zoosk. This can lead to emotional harm and, in some cases, identity theft or financial scams. Users are advised to verify identities and avoid sharing personal information too quickly

- **Data Privacy Concerns:** Several dating platforms have experienced data breaches, raising concerns about the security of user information. High-profile incidents like the Ashley Madison hack highlighted the risks of sharing personal data on dating sites.

- **Safety Risks During In-Person Meetings:** While most in-person meetings are safe, there have been cases of assault and other crimes. Users are encouraged to take precautions, such as meeting in public places and informing friends or family about their plans.

Top 10 Safe Dating Sites

1. **eHarmony:** Known for its focus on long-term relationships and compatibility, eHarmony uses a comprehensive questionnaire and matching system. Its robust security measures include profile verification and active monitoring for fake profiles.
2. **Match.com:** As one of the oldest dating sites, Match.com is recognized for its detailed profiles and robust safety features, including background checks and options to avoid sharing personal contact information early on.
3. **ChristianMingle:** This platform offers a safe space for those seeking faith-based relationships. It has rigorous security measures, including photo verification and automatic flagging of suspicious activity, which helps maintain a respectful environment.
4. **Bumble:** Bumble's safety features include a verification process where users match specific poses in selfies, a Safety Center with resources for handling online harassment, and a "ladies first" messaging feature to give women more control.
5. **The League:** The League is an exclusive app that thoroughly vets its members through LinkedIn and other social media profiles. It is designed for high-achieving professionals and provides a secure, curated environment.

6. **OkCupid:** This app offers comprehensive profiles and matches based on a detailed questionnaire. It strongly focuses on inclusivity and allows for extensive profile customization and message filtering to avoid unwanted interactions.
7. **Hily:** Hily uses AI to improve matches and has safety features like a risk score for users. It focuses on secure, data-driven interactions and offers resources to ensure user safety and privacy.
8. **Zoosk:** Zoosk has a broad user base and employs photo verification and behavioral matchmaking technology to create a safer experience. It is well-regarded for its diverse membership and active moderation.
9. **SeniorMatch:** Designed for singles over 50, SeniorMatch has a straightforward verification process and caters to those seeking serious relationships. It also offers privacy features, such as the ability to hide profiles.
10. **BlackPeopleMeet:** This site is tailored for Black and biracial singles. It utilizes profile and photo verification, offering various safety features to protect its members, making it a reputable choice for niche dating.

Top 10 Dating Sites to Avoid

1. **Ashley Madison:** Known for its focus on extramarital affairs, Ashley Madison has faced numerous security breaches, including a high-profile hack that exposed user information. Its reputation for security and privacy remains a concern.
2. **AdultFriendFinder:** This site has experienced several data breaches and has been criticized for the high number of fake profiles and scams. It is not recommended for those seeking a secure and genuine dating experience.
3. **Tinder:** While popular, Tinder has issues with fake profiles, scams, and harassment. It is often used for casual dating, attracting unwanted interactions, and reducing users' safety.
4. **Grindr:** This dating app for LGBTQ+ individuals has faced multiple security and privacy issues, including the exposure of user locations. It is known for its limited verification and safety features.
5. **Plenty of Fish:** POF is criticized for the high number of fake profiles and scammers. Its security features are less robust than those of other platforms, making it easier for malicious users to target others.

6. **Seeking.com:** Formerly known as Seeking Arrangement, this site is geared towards "sugar dating," which can attract individuals with questionable intentions. It has faced criticism for its high membership fees and lack of transparency.
7. **Badoo:** Badoo has been criticized for its lack of effective moderation and the presence of many fake profiles. It is not recommended for those seeking severe or safe dating experiences.
8. **Feeld:** While promoting openness and inclusivity, Feeld's focus on alternative relationships can attract users with diverse intentions, and its limited user base and verification features may not be ideal for those seeking security.
9. **Whiplr:** This app for BDSM and kink communities has been criticized for poor user verification and a high number of fake profiles. It lacks sufficient security measures to ensure user safety.
10. **Happn:** Although Happn uses location-based matching, its security features are less robust than other platforms. It has faced issues with user privacy and unwanted advances, making it less safe than other options.

These recommendations are based on reviews of security features, user experiences, and the presence of scams or fake profiles. For more details, refer to sources like DatingAdvice.com, DatingNews.com, Healthy Framework, and mindbodygreen.

While online dating can be a great way to meet people, it's essential to remain vigilant and use platforms that prioritize user safety. Researching different sites, reading reviews, and understanding the pros and cons can help you choose a dating app that aligns with your needs and expectations.

Sources:
- https://staysafe.org/cyber-safety-tips-for-adults/
- https://usa.kaspersky.com/resource-center/preemptive-safety/top-10-internet-safety-rules-and-what-not-to-do-online
- https://www.keepersecurity.com/blog/2022/09/27/7-tips-for-staying-safe-on-social-media/
- https://www.ncsc.gov.uk/guidance/social-media-how-to-use-it-safely
- https://www.cisa.gov/news-events/news/staying-safe-social-networking-sites
- https://www.eharmony.ca/dating-advice/dating/the-pros-and-cons-of-online-dating/

- https://healthyframework.com/zoosk-review/
- https://www.pewresearch.org/internet/2020/02/06/the-virtues-and-downsides-of-online-dating/
- https://onlineforlove.com/online-dating-pros-cons/
- https://tawkify.com/blog/dating-methods/best-dating-apps-sites-seattle
- https://www.mindbodygreen.com/articles/best-dating-sites
- https://www.forbes.com/health/dating/best-online-dating-websites/
- https://www.datingnews.com/industry-trends/best-free-dating-sites/
- https://www.datingadvice.com/
- https://healthyframework.com/
- https://www.mindbodygreen.com/articles/questions-to-ask-on-dating-app
- FBI - Elder Fraud Report
- AARP - Online Dating Scams
- FTC - Romance Scams

Use What You Got

At the time of an attack with defend with resistance

Defensive resistance techniques are actions to avoid or deter an attacker, such as running, yelling, or physical maneuvers to escape a potentially dangerous situation.

Running:
- Description: Quickly moving away from a threat to put distance between yourself and the attacker.
- Purpose: It increases your chance of safety by creating space, allowing you to seek help or find a safe location.
- When to Use: If you can safely run to a public place or a location where other people can assist.

Yelling or Shouting:
- Description: Loudly calling out for help, saying things like "Help!", "Fire!", "You're Not my Boyfriend," or "Call the police!"
- Purpose: Attracts attention to your situation, which can deter an attacker and summon assistance from nearby people.

- **When to Use:** In a public or semi-public area where people might hear and respond.

Physical Techniques:
- Striking Sensitive Areas: Targeting areas such as the eyes, nose, throat, or groin to incapacitate the attacker temporarily.
- Purpose: To cause enough pain or distraction to allow you to escape.
- When to Use: You must physically defend yourself if escape isn't immediately possible.

Creating Barriers:
- Description: Using objects or barriers to slow down or block an attacker.
- Purpose: It provides a physical shield and time to plan your next move or call for help.
- When to Use: If you can position yourself behind a door, a piece of furniture, or any obstacle.

Using Your Environment:
- Description: Utilizing objects around you, such as keys, pens, or even dirt, as tools or weapons.
- Purpose: To distract, disorient, or hurt an attacker long enough for you to escape.
- When to Use: When near an attacker, you have quick access to an object.

Defensive Posture:
- Description: Standing in a way that protects vital areas and prepares you for potential impact or defence.
- Purpose: To minimize injury and signal the attacker that you are prepared to defend yourself.
- When to Use: When confrontation seems unavoidable.

These techniques are most effective when combined with awareness and intuition about your surroundings and situation. The goal is always to prioritize safety and escape over confrontation whenever possible.

Lethal and Non-Lethal Weapons

The rules and regulations surrounding the use of lethal and non-lethal weapons for self-defense can be complex and vary widely depending on the location. Understanding these laws is crucial for anyone who wishes to protect themselves legally and responsibly in the event of an attack.

Being informed can significantly affect your safety and legal standing, whether you carry a firearm, use pepper spray, or know your rights in a dangerous situation. This guide provides an overview of the general principles of self-defense, the types of weapons that may be available, and the contexts in which you can legally defend yourself.

The rules surrounding the use of lethal and non-lethal weapons for self-defense vary greatly depending on the country, state, or jurisdiction. Here are some general principles:

Principles of Self-Defense
- **Reasonable Force:** Self-defense generally allows using reasonable force to protect oneself from imminent harm. The force used must be proportionate to the threat faced.
- **Imminent Threat:** The threat must be immediate. You can only use force to defend yourself if you believe you are in immediate danger.
- **Duty to Retreat**: Some places have a "duty to retreat" rule, requiring you to avoid confrontation if possible. Others have "Stand Your Ground" laws, which allow you to defend yourself without retreating.
- **Castle Doctrine**: Many places allow the use of force, including lethal force, to defend oneself in one's home (and sometimes one's vehicle or workplace).

Lethal Weapons
- Firearms: You need a firearm permit in many places. The use of firearms for self-defense is heavily regulated. Some areas require the gun to be concealed, while others permit open carry.
- Knives: Laws regarding knives vary. Carrying specific knives (e.g., switchblades, butterfly knives) is prohibited in some places, and blade length is often restricted.
- Other Weapons: Some brass knuckles, batons, or martial arts weapons may be regulated or prohibited.

Non-Lethal Weapons
- Pepper Spray/Mace: These are generally legal for self-defence, but there may be restrictions on the size or strength of the spray. Some places require a permit.
- Tasers/Stun Guns are legal in many places but may require a permit. Some jurisdictions prohibit their use entirely.
- Personal Alarms: These are legal and generally encouraged for self-defence. They emit a loud noise to deter attackers and alert others.
- **Self-Defense Keychains:** Items like Kubota or tactical pens are legal but may be subject to weapons laws in certain jurisdictions.

Availability During an Attack
- Preparedness: Knowing local laws and having legal self-defense tools readily available is essential.
- Carry Restrictions: Some locations, such as government buildings, schools, or airplanes, restrict what you can carry.
- Improvised Weapons: In an emergency, everyday objects (e.g., keys, umbrellas) can be used for defense if you are not carrying a designated weapon.

Where You Can Use Self-Defense
- **Public Places:** You have the right to defend yourself in public places if attacked, but the force used must be reasonable and necessary.
- **Private Property:** Laws like the Castle Doctrine allow more leeway for self-defense in your home.
- **Restricted Areas:** Airports, courthouses, and schools often prohibit the carrying of weapons, even for self-defense.

Specific Considerations
- **Training and Safety:** Proper training is advisable, especially for firearms or other lethal weapons.
- **Legal Consequences:** The use of force, especially lethal force, can lead to legal repercussions, including criminal charges or civil lawsuits.

Always check local laws and regulations to understand what is permissible in your area.

Everyday Items Can Be Used for Defense

In the event of a home invasion or unexpected attack, it's crucial to be aware of everyday items in your surroundings that can be used for self-defense. While specialized weapons may not always be accessible, everyday household objects can be practical tools for protecting yourself and your loved ones.

Each room in your home contains unique items that can be repurposed for defense, from kitchen utensils and living room furniture to bathroom fixtures and garage tools. This guide explores the potential defensive uses of various household objects, helping you understand how to turn your immediate environment into a means of safeguarding yourself in a crisis.

Use what you got – Look around

Depending on your room, various everyday objects can be used in a home for self-defence. Here's a breakdown of potential items you could use in each room:

Living Room
- **Lamps**: Can be used as a blunt object for striking.
- **Fireplace Tools**: Poker, shovel, or brush can be used to strike or defend.
- **Heavy Decorations**: Items like vases, sculptures, or picture frames can be used to throw or as blunt instruments.
- **Furniture**: Cushions or small tables can block or deflect attacks.

Kitchen
- **Knives**: Knives are readily available, but their use should be carefully considered due to their lethal potential.
- **Heavy Pots and Pans**: Good for striking.
- **Utensils**: Forks or rolling pins can be used for jabbing or striking.
- **Spices**: Throwing chili powder, pepper, or other irritants can temporarily disable an attacker.
- **Bug Spray or Cleaners**: These can be sprayed into someone's eyes or face.

Bedroom
- **Heavy Objects**: Books, alarm clocks, or lamps can be used for striking.
- **Belt or Clothing**: Belts can be used for swinging or constriction, and clothing like scarves can be used to entangle or distract.
- **Bed Frame or Headboard**: Detachable pieces or parts of furniture can be used as defensive tools.
- **Sprays or Lotions**: Perfume or hairspray, cleaning and bug sprays can irritate the eyes.

Bathroom
- **Cleaning Supplies**: Bleach or other strong chemicals can be used as irritants.
- **Towel Rack or Shower Rod**: Can be pulled down and used as a striking tool.

- **Toilet Tank Lid**: Heavy and solid, can be used as a blunt weapon.
- **Personal Grooming Tools**: Items like hairbrushes, scissors, or razors can be used defensively.

Garage
- **Tools**: Hammers, wrenches, or screwdrivers can be used for striking or stabbing.
- **Sports Equipment**: Bats, hockey sticks, or golf clubs are effective for striking.
- **Chemicals**: Paints, solvents, or insect sprays can be thrown or sprayed.
- **Car Keys**: Can be used to strike vulnerable areas.

Office/Study
- **Office Supplies**: Scissors, letter openers, or staplers can be improvised weapons.
- **Books**: Large, heavy books can be thrown or used for striking.
- **Electronic Devices**: Laptops or keyboards can be used as blunt objects.
- **Sprays**: Cleaners and Air Freshers

Hallways or Entryways
- **Umbrellas or Canes**: Good for striking or blocking.
- **Shoes**: Hard-soled shoes can be used to strike.

- **Coat Racks or Hooks**: These can disarm or trip an attacker.

General Tips:
- **Improvised Shields**: Anything large enough to act as a barrier (like a cushion, tray, or small table) can shield against an attacker.
- **Escape Routes**: Always be aware of exits and possible escape routes in each room.
- **Communication Tools**: Phones, intercoms, or smart devices to call for help.

Weapons On Your Body

Your Body is a powerful tool for Fighting

Understanding which parts of your body can be used as weapons and how to use them effectively can be crucial in a dangerous situation. Here are the primary personal weapons on your body:

Voice: Yelling: Shouting can startle an attacker, attract attention, and alert others to your situation.

Head
- Headbutt: Using the hard part of your forehead to strike an assailant's nose or face can be effective, especially in close quarters.

Teeth
- Biting: Biting can be a last-resort defense to inflict pain and potentially break free from an attacker in a choke hold, but other techniques are more impactful.

Hands and Fingers
- **Fists:** Can be used for punching vulnerable areas like the face, throat, or solar plexus.
- **Palm Heel**: Striking with the heel of your palm can be effective against the nose or chin, reducing the risk of injury to your hand.
- **Fingers:** Jabbing or gouging with your fingers can target sensitive areas such as the eyes, throat, or soft tissue.

Elbows
- **Elbow Strikes:** The elbow is one of the most vital parts of your body. With significant force, it can strike the face, ribs, or torso in close combat.

Forearms
- **Blocks and Strikes:** The forearms can block incoming attacks or deliver strong blows to an assailant's neck or head.

Legs and Feet
- Knees: If the attacker is bent, the knee can be used in close-range attacks, such as striking the groin, stomach, or face.
- Feet: Kicking with the ball, heel, or side of your foot can be effective against the shins, knees, or groin. A stomping motion can also target the attacker's foot or ankle.

Hips and Shoulders
- Body Checks: Using your hips or shoulders to push or check an attacker can create space or disrupt their balance.

Knowing how to use these body parts effectively and basic self-defense techniques can improve your chances of escaping or deterring an attack. Always remember that the goal of self-defense is to create an opportunity to flee to safety.

Vulnerable locations on the Body

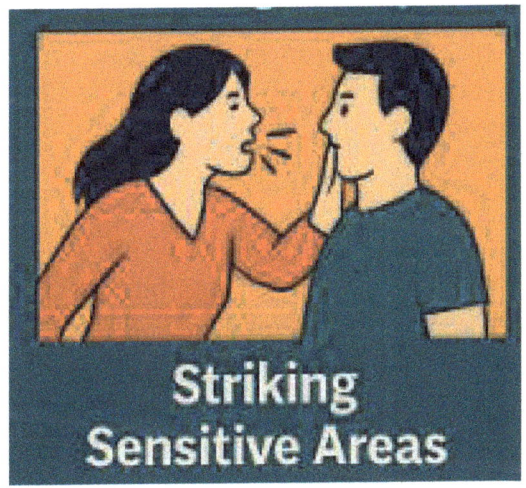

Knowing where to strike can be as important as knowing how to hit in self-defense. When targeted, the human body has several vulnerable areas that can cause significant pain, disorientation, or temporary incapacitation, providing a crucial opportunity to escape or protect oneself.

Whether you are facing an assailant much stronger than you or just need to neutralize a threat quickly, understanding these key points — such as the eyes, throat, and groin — can maximize the effectiveness of your defensive actions.

Below are the most sensitive locations on the body to strike during an attack, empowering you to respond swiftly and strategically in a dangerous situation. Targeting vulnerable locations on an attacker's body can maximize the effectiveness of your strikes and help you escape a dangerous situation. These areas are more sensitive and can cause significant pain or temporary incapacitation.

Head and Neck
- **Eyes**: Striking or gouging the eyes can cause severe pain and temporary blindness, giving you a chance to escape.
- **Nose**: A punch or palm strike to the nose can cause intense pain, disorientation, and even temporary vision impairment due to tearing.
- **Throat**: The throat is extremely sensitive. Striking here can cause difficulty breathing, coughing, or choking.
- **Jaw and Chin**: A decisive strike to the jaw can disorient an attacker or even cause a knockout.
- **Temple**: This area is susceptible; a strike here can cause disorientation or unconsciousness.
- **Ears**: Slapping or cupping the ears can cause pain and disorientation due to the disrupted balance and the sensitive eardrum.

Torso
- **Solar Plexus**: Located in the upper abdomen, a strike here can knock the wind out of an attacker, causing them to double over and struggle to breathe.
- **Ribs**: A powerful strike to the ribs can cause significant pain, difficulty breathing, and even fractures.
- **Kidneys**: Located in the lower back, a strike to the kidneys can cause intense pain and shock, potentially incapacitating the attacker.
- **Diaphragm**: A strike below the ribs can cause the diaphragm to spasm, making it hard for the attacker to breathe.

Look for areas where bones meet at the "joint" to strike.

Groin
- **Genitals**: A strike to the groin area, especially for male attackers, can cause extreme pain and temporary incapacitation. This is one of the most effective areas to target in close-quarters defence.

Limbs
- **Knees**: Kicking the side or back of the knee can destabilize an attacker, causing them to lose balance or fall.

- **Shins**: The shinbone is sensitive to pain. A firm kick or strike can cause significant discomfort and disrupt an attacker's movement.
- **Top of Foot or Instep**: Stomping on the top of an attacker's foot can cause pain and limit their ability to pursue you.

Hands and Fingers
- **Fingers**: Bending or twisting the fingers can cause pain and help break an attacker's grip.
- **Wrist**: Striking or twisting the wrist can make an attacker release a weapon or loosen their hold.

Targeting these vulnerable areas can increase the effectiveness of your self-defense techniques, allowing you to incapacitate or disorient an attacker long enough to escape to safety. Always strike with the intent to defend yourself and seek help immediately.

Explaining Grab Targets

Here are the most effective anatomical targets working from Head to Toes to free yourself from a variety of common hand-grab scenarios:

1. Wrist Grabs
- **Thumb Base:** The thumb is the weakest part of the grip. To break hold, pinch, pull, or strike at the fleshy web between the thumb and index finger. Work the C where the fingers meet.
- **Radial Nerve (Inner Forearm):** A chop or jab about two inches above the wrist on the thumb side can shock the nerve and loosen the grip.

2. Two-Handed Wrist Holds
- **Elbow to Forearm:** Bring your free elbow down sharply into the attacker's forearm, just below the wrist, targeting the radius bone or the muscle belly.
- **Knee Strike:** If you're close enough, a forceful knee into the groin or lower thigh can force them to release your arms.
- **Foot Stomp:** Stomping on the top of a foot can cause pain and limit their ability to pursue you.

3. Bear-Hug Grabs (From Front or Rear)
- **Solar Plexus/Upper Abdomen:** A palm-heel strike or elbow into the solar plexus can knock the wind out of them, forcing them to loosen their hold.
- **Groin:** A decisive thrust to the groin—even through clothing—can break their focus and give you space to escape.
- **Foot Stomp (Instep):** Stomp down hard on the top of their foot to induce pain and distract them.

4. Clothing Grabs (Shirt, Jacket)
- **Thumb Web:** Ripping at the thumb web often works, as above.
- **Face (Eyes/Nose):** If they're directly in front of you, quick jabs to the eyes or a palm strike to the nose can force them to back off.

5. Headlocks & Choke Holds
- **Throat:** Strike or palm-heel the throat to interrupt their breathing or grip.
- **Temple/Jaw:** A sharp strike to the side of the head can disorient them and break their tunnel vision.
- **Spine/Back of Head:** A back-of-the-head hammer fist or elbow can break their leverage if you can reach.

6. Hair Grabs

- **Secure your head:** Use both hands to hold the attacker's hand that is grabbing your hair. This will help reduce the pain and prevent them from pulling your hair further.

- **Create a base:** Lower your center of gravity by bending your knees slightly and widening your stance. This will provide you with more stability and make it more difficult for the attacker to control you.

- **Strike vulnerable areas:** Use your free hand to strike the attacker's vulnerable areas, such as the eyes, nose, throat, or groin. This will cause pain and create an opportunity for you to escape.

- **Turn and pull**: Turn your body in the direction of the attacker's thumb, as this is the weakest part of their grip. Pull your head away from their hand while continuing to strike their vulnerable areas.

- **Escape**: Once you have broken free from the hair grab, create distance between you and the attacker and seek help immediately.

On the Ground

When you end up on the ground, your priority is to re-establish distance and prevent the attacker from landing effective strikes or taking control. Here are key tactics:

1. Protect Your Head and Vital Areas
- **Cover Up:** Tuck your chin, raise your forearms, and keep your elbows in to shield your head, throat, and torso.
- **Sprawl Your Legs:** Extend one leg straight back to prevent the attacker from closing in and use the other to "post" (plant foot to create space).

2. Create Space with Shrimping (Hip Escape)
- **Hip Escape:** Lie on your back, turn onto one shoulder, plant your foot, and thrust your hips away from the attacker. This "shrimp" motion creates a wedge of space between you and them.
- **Repetition:** Repeat on each side until you gain enough room to sit up or kick them away.

3. Use Up-Kicks and Push Kicks
- **Up-Kick:** On your back, bend one knee and thrust your foot upward into the attacker's midsection or groin, then switch legs.

- **Push Kick (Foot to Face):** If they're over you, thrust both feet forward to their hips or chest to shove them back.

4. Transition to Guard Positions
- **Closed Guard:** Wrap your legs around their waist, lock your ankles, and control their posture by pulling down on their shoulders or collar bone.
- **Half Guard:** Trap one leg between yours as they try to pass; use your arms to control a wrist or bicep.
- **Open Guard Variations:** Use hooks (feet on their thighs or hips) to off-balance them while you work to stand or better position yourself.

5. Break Their Posture
- **Grip Their Collar or Shoulders:** Pull them forward to disrupt their balance.
- **Elbow Control:** Grip their wrist and pull it across their body — this destabilizes them and limits their striking.

6. Work Your Way Up
- **Technical Stand-Up:** From a seated posture, place one hand behind you, one foot on the ground, and the opposite knee up; lift your hips and bring your free leg underneath you, returning to your feet without exposing your back.

- **Rotate and Stand:** As you shrimp and control one side, rotate your hips to face them, plant a foot, and drive up into a squat or stand.

7. Use What's at Hand
- **Improvised Barriers:** If there's a bag, jacket, or chair nearby, bring it between you and the attacker as you recover.
- **Environment:** Shift your position toward walls, furniture edges, or a window to limit their angles of attack.

Remember: On the ground, time is critical. Strike quickly, create space, protect your head, and stand as soon as it's safe to do so. Practice these movements slowly at first, then build speed and decisiveness, so they become instinctive under stress.

Firearms and Knives

When someone attacks you with a firearm or knife, your priority is survival—keeping distance, de-escalating, and escaping if possible.

Disarming or fighting techniques are extremely high-risk and should only be attempted as a last resort (e.g., if you're being threatened in a confined space and there is no chance to flee or call for help).

1. Verbal De-Escalation & Compliance
- **Use a calm, firm voice:** "I don't want any trouble. Take what you want and leave me alone."
- **Avoid sudden movements:** Keep your hands visible and your body language nonthreatening.
- **Buy time:** Stall— "Here's my wallet"—to look for an opening to flee or draw attention.

2. Create Distance & Seek Cover
- **Back away slowly:** Try to put obstacles (cars, furniture, pillars) between you and the weapon.
- **Use improvised shields:** A bag, jacket, chair, or trash can lid can block or slow a blade or bullet.
- **Get to a safer angle:** Move diagonally behind cover so the attacker can't aim straight at you.

3. Distraction & Escape
- **Throw an object:** Keys, purse, or water bottle toward their face or feet to force them to flinch or look away.
- **Shout for help:** Attract witnesses—a loud noise can startle an armed attacker and invite intervention.
- **Run to safety:** Once they're distracted, sprint to a secure location, calling 911 as you go.

4. Close-Range Disarm (Last Resort)
Only if cornered

- **Make the Attacker Feel Like You Are Giving Up. Talk To Them, say, " Ok, Ok, Ok while moving your hands to distract.**
- **Knife-hand control:** Strike the attacker's knife hand wrist with a hammer fist or palm-heel to force release.
- **Gun barrel redirect:** Use both hands to push the barrel up sharply while simultaneously stepping offline—then twist the weapon out of their grip and run.
- **Target the weapon hand:** Elbow-strike or hammer-fist the attacker's wrist or forearm to weaken their grip on the weapon.

5. Target Vulnerable Areas
- **Eyes/Throat:** A quick gouge to the eyes or a palm-heel strike to the throat can shock them and let you escape.

- **Groin/Solar Plexus:** A forceful knee or elbow here can buy crucial seconds if you're close enough.

6. Post-Event Actions
- **Put distance:** Get as far away as possible before tending to injuries.
- **Call 911 immediately:** Provide your location, a description of the attacker, and the weapon.
- **Preserve evidence:** Don't wash blood or wipe surfaces—this can help police.

Remember: Your best defense is awareness and avoidance. Whenever you see an armed attacker, compliance and creating space are far safer than trying to disarm them—fight only if you have no other choice.

Key Principle: Always "hit hard, hit fast," targeting whatever vulnerable point is accessible, then move immediately to escape, toward safety, help, or a secure location.

Summary Posters for Printing or Sharing

Common Sense Safety for Women

We Can Learn to Live Safely as Mothers, Wives, and Business Professionals in a Man's World!

Using Common Sense for Self-Defense

All Images generated by OpenAI's DALL·E [Large language model] (2024 & 2025) unless noted

GENERAL LESSONS ACROSS ALL BOOKS

PSYCHOLOGICAL INSIGHTS

Understand the psychology behind predatory behavior

BEHAVIORAL INDICATORS

Recognizing early warning signs and behavioral indicators

IMPORTANCE OF EDUCATION

The crucial role of educating public, especially vulnerable groups, on recognizing and preventing

SUPPORT SYSTEMS

Providing support systems and assistance to those affected by predatory actions

UNDERSTANDING SELF-DEFENSE LAW

PRINCIPLES OF SELF-DEFENSE LAW

Reasonable Belief
You must reasonably believe you are in imminent danger of harm.

Proportional Response
The force used in self-defense must be proportional to the threat

Duty to Retreat (Varies by State)
Some states require you to retreat if possible before using force

Castle Doctrine
Right to use force to defend your home against unlawful entry

DOMESTIC VIOLENCE CONSIDERATIONS

Context and History
Patterns of abuse can impact legal proceedings

Imminence of Threat
Ongoing nature of abuse affects threat assessment

No Duty to Retreat
May not be required to retreat in your own home

Protective Orders
Violations by the abuser can support self-defense

Laws vary by jurisdiction. Knowing your rights can empower appropriate action in

SECURITY IN YOUR HOME, APARTMENT, OR HOTEL ROOM

DOORS

- Reinforce doors
- Consider a peephole or video doorbell
- Put a lock on each door

WINDOWS

- Cover windows
- Secure sliding doors and windows
- Avoid leaving windows open when unattended

MULTI-FLOOR BUILDINGS

- Be aware of common areas
- Use well-lit building entrances

LODGING SAFETY

- Research accommodations
- Ensure secure locks

GENERAL SAFETY

 Lock doors & windows   Get to know neighbors   Secure valuables

10 BURGLARS SECRETS
Insider tips to protect your home

 Your routine is intel
Watchers learn when you're gone.

 Unlocked = open invite
Lock doors/windows; ditch spare keys.

 Neglected yard says 'away'
Tidy up; pause mail & packages.

 Security signs deter
Stickers, alarms, cameras reduduce risk.

 Master bedroom is first
Hide valuables essehwere.

 Speed is the plan
Lights, strong locks, alarms slow me.

 I stalk your socials
Share trips after you're back

 I hunt weak spots
Bright lights, good locks, cameras.

SMART SAFETY AROUND YOUR CAR

PLAN YOUR ROUTE

KEYS IN HAND

LOCKING & SECURING YOUR CAR

INSPECT THE AREA

SHARE YOUR WHEREABOUTS

PARKING SAFETY

KEY MANAGEMENT

DRESS FOR SAFETY

Taxi & Rideshare Safety Tips

VERIFY YOUR DRIVER

SIT IN THE BACK SEAT

SHARE YOUR TRIP DETAILS

MONITOR THE ROUTE

MAINTAIN PROFESSIONAL BOUNDARIES

USE EMERGENCY FEATURES

EXIT SAFELY

KEEP KEYS AND ESSENTIALS HANDY

CARRY PESONAL DEFENSE ITEMS

DRESS FOR AGILITY

GENERAL TRAVEL SAFETY

DRESS TO BLEND IN

STAY SOBER AND ALERT

TRUST YOUR INSTINCTS

SECURE YOUR BELONGINGS

MINIMIZE PUBLIC MAPS & GUIDEBOOKS

LIMIT OVERSHARING

HAVE EMERGENCY CONTACTS HANDY

CONSIDERING COMPLIANCE IN VIOLENT SITUATIONS

PRESERVATION OF LIFE

The goal is to survive and reduce the risk of further harm

UNDERSTAND THE SITUATION

Consider if the attacker is armed or behaving errattically

BUYING TIME

Complying may provide a chance to plan an escape

AVOID FURTHER INJURY

Resistance could escalate the level of violence

PSYCHOLOGICAL IMPACT

Compliance is a survival response, not an indication of consent

SEEK HELP

Report the crime and pursue medical and legal assistance

ENSURE YOUR PRIVACY, PREVENT HARASSMENT, AND SECURE YOUR DIGITAL LIFE

ONLINE FINANCIAL SAFETY

- Create strong unique passwords
- Enable two-factor authentication

LIMIT USE OF PUBLIC WI-FI

- Limit use of public Wi-Fi for financial transactions

BE WARY OF PHISHING SCAMS

- Keep software updated

ONLINE CREDIT CARDS VS. DEBIT CARDS

- Dispute resolution
- Better fraud protection
- Rewards
- Immediate impact on funds

SAFETY TIPS USING CREDIT AND DEBIT CARDS

- Enable alerts
- Limit debit card use
- Monitor statements regularly

CYBERBULLYING: WOMEN VS. MEN

41% OF AMERICANS HAVE EXPERIENCED ONLINE HARASSMENT

26% PHYSICAL THREATS OR SEXUAL HARASSMENT

WOMEN VS. MEN

16% ↑ SEXUALLY HARASSED

35% CALLED OFFENSIVE NAMES

STEPS TO TAKE

- DO NOT ENGAGE
- DOCUMENT EVERYTHING
- REPORT ABUSE
- BLOCK THE BULLY

ONLINE DATING SAFETY TIPS

 **USE REPUTABLE DATING SITES/APPS**

KEEP PERSONAL INFORMATION PRIVATE

VERIFY THEIR IDENTITY

 **MEET IN PUBLIC PLACES**

 **INFORM A FRIEND OR FAMILY MEMBER**

TRUST YOUR INSTINCTS

 **BE AWARE OF SCAMS**

 LIMIT ONLINE COMMUNICATION

DEFEND BY RESISTANCE

Running or Moving Away

Yelling or Shouting

Striking Sensitive Areas

Make Barriers or Shields

Escape Routes

Safety Tools

Using Environment

Use What is Available

UPPER BODY WEAPONS

Head

Headbutt
Using the hard part of your forehead to strike an assailant's nose or face can be effective, especially in close quarters.

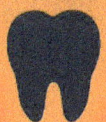

Teeth

Biting
Biting can be a last-resort defense to inflict pain and potentially break free from an attacker in a choke hold, but other techniques are more impactful.

Hands and Fingers

Fists
Can be used for punching vulnerable areas like the face, throat, or solar plexus.

Palm Heel
Striking with the heel of your palm can be effective against the nose or chin, reducing the risk of injury to your hard.

Elbows

Elbow Strikes
The elbow is one of the most vital parts of your body. With significant force, it can strike the tace, ribs, or torso in close combat.

Upper Body Weapons

Lower Body Weapons

Legs and Feet

Knees:
If the attacker is bent, the knee can be used in close-range attacks, such as striking the groin, stomach, or face.

Feet:
Kicking with the ball, heel or side of your foot can be effective against the shins, knees, or groin.

Hips and Shoulders

Body Checks:
Using your hips or shoulders to push or check an attacker can create space or disrupt their balance.

KEY PRINCIPLE

ALWAYS 'HIT HARD, HIT FAST,' targeting whatever vulnerable point is accessible, then move immediately to escape, toward safety, help, or a secure location

Look for areas where bones meet at the "joint" to strike.

Groin

Genitals: A strike to the groin area, especially for male attackers, can cause extreme pain and temporary incapacitation.

This is one of the most effective areas to target in close-quarters defence.

Limbs

Knees: Kicking the side or back of the knee can destabilize an attacker, causing them to lose balance or fall.

Shins: The shinbone is sensitive to pain. A firm kick or strike can cause significant discomfort and disrupt an attacker's movement.

Top of Foot or Instep: Stomping on the top of an attacker's foot can cause pain and limit their ability to pursue you.

Hands and Fingers

Fingers: Bending or twisting the fingers can cause pain and help break an attacker's grip.

Wrist: striking or twisting the wrist can make an attacker release a weapon or loosen their hold.

GETTING OUT OF GRABS

The thumb is the weakest part of the grip. To break the hold pinch, pull or strike at the fleshy web between the thumb end index finger. Work the "C" where

WORK THE C

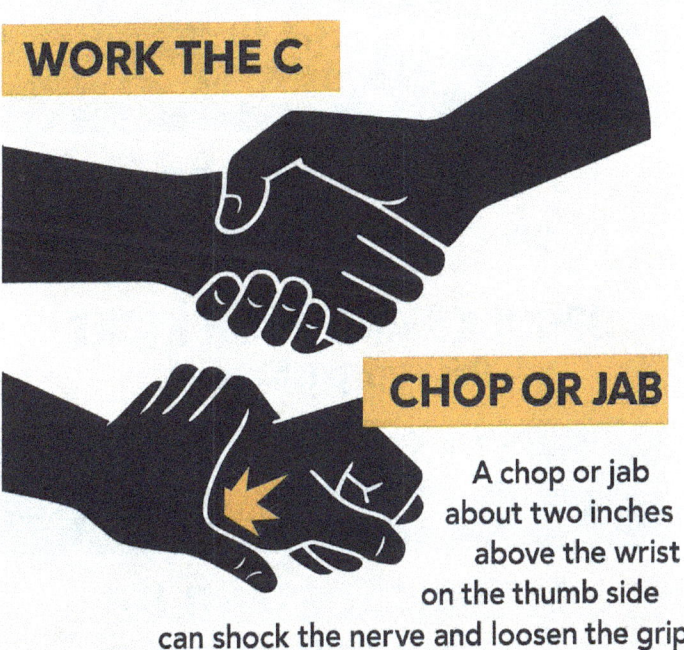

CHOP OR JAB

A chop or jab about two inches above the wrist on the thumb side can shock the nerve and loosen the grip

SELF-DEFENSE TACTICS WHEN KNOCKED TO THE GROUND

PROTECT HEAD AND VITAL AREAS
(cover up, sprawl legs)

HIP ESCAPE
(create space)

BREAK POSTURE
(pull forward, control arms)

UP-KICKS AND PUSH KICKS
(kick up, push away)

GUARD POSITIONS
(closed, half, open)

TECHNICAL STAND-UP
(rotate hips, rise to stand

References – Books and Websites

1. Challenges Faced by Women (1970s–1990s)

> **Domestic Violence & Legal Protections**
> – NCADV, "Domestic Violence." NCADV. Retrieved from NCADV
> – Violence Against Women Act (VAWA) of 1994. U.S. Congress. Available at Congress.gov

- **Business Travel**
  – Fels, A. (2004). *Necessary Dreams: Ambition in Women's Changing Lives*. Harvard University Press.
  – Babin, B. J. & Boles, J. S. (1996). "Co-worker involvement & supervisor support…" *Journal of Retailing*.

- **Rural vs. Urban Violence**
  – Logan, T. K., Walker, R. & Hoyt, W. (2012). "The Rural Context…" *Trauma, Violence, & Abuse*, 13(3), 201–221.
  – Peek-Asa, C. et al. (2011). "Rural disparity in domestic violence…" *Journal of Women's Health*, 20(11), 1743–1749.

- **Intersection of Race & IPV**
  – CDC, NISVS 2010–12 State Report. Available at CDC NISVS
  – Richie, B. E. (2012). *Arrested Justice: Black Women, Violence, and America's Prison Nation*. NYU Press.

- **Religious-Institution Abuse**
  – Browne, A. & Finkelhor, D. (1986). "Impact of Child Sexual Abuse…" *Psychological Bulletin*, 99(1), 66–77.
  – Finkelhor, D. & Williams, L. M. (1988). *License to Rape: Sexual Abuse of Wives*. Free Press.

- **Violence in Sports**
  – USA Gymnastics Abuse Scandal: public reports & court documents.
  – Kerr, G., Willson, E. & Stirling, A. (2020). "The Safe Sport Movement…" *International Review for the Sociology of Sport*, 55(5), 555–574.

2. Books on Fear & Self-Defense

- Jeffers, S. L., *Feel the Fear and Do It Anyway*

- de Becker, G., *The Gift of Fear*

- Bishop, G. J., *Unfuk Yourself**

- Kardian, S., *The New Superpower for Women*

- Larkin, T., *When Violence Is the Answer*

3. Self-Defense Law & Support Resources

- **Law Overviews**
  - Cornell LII, Self-Defense
  - NCSL, Stand Your Ground & Castle Doctrine

- **Domestic Violence & VAWA**
  - ABA Commission on Domestic & Sexual Violence: americanbar.org
  - National Domestic Violence Hotline: thehotline.org
  - DOJ, Office on Violence Against Women: justice.gov/ovw
  - White House Fact Sheet on VAWA Reauthorization: whitehouse.gov

- **General Legal Aid**
  - Legal Aid Society: legalaid.org
  - FindLaw, Self-Defense Overview

4. Workplace & School Violence Prevention

- **Federal Laws & Guidelines**
  - OSHA, Violence Prevention for Healthcare & Social Service Workers
  - EEOC, Title VII Guidance
  - ADA Regulations & Guidance: ada.gov

- **State Laws**
  - Cal/OSHA Healthcare Violence Prevention Law
  - NY Workplace Violence Prevention Act

- **Sector-Specific Data & Programs**
  - NCES, School Safety Reports
  - APA, Violence in Schools & Healthcare
  - ANA, Nursing Workplace Violence Resources
  - NEA, School Safety Resources
  - Kaiser Permanente Violence Prevention Strategies
  - NYC DOE Anti-Violence Initiative
  - UTMB BERT Program Overview

5. Cyberbullying Resources

- StopBullying.gov
- PACER National Bullying Prevention Center
- Cyberbullying Research Center
- Common Sense Media
- Child Mind Institute
- Netsmartz (NCMEC)
- The Trevor Project
- Stomp Out Bullying

6. Misc. Online Safety & Risk Resources

- https://www.domesticviolenceinfo.ca/resources
- https://just2seconds.org/
- https://advisorsmith.com/data/most-dangerous-jobs/
- https://www.insurdinary.ca/what-are-the-most-dangerous-jobs-in-canada/
- https://info.apartmentguardian.com/blog/is-working-in-real-estate-dangerous-heres-what-the-statistics-say
- https://www.paloaltoonline.com/real-estate/2023/09/20/showing-property-can-be-a-dangerous-job/
- https://propertyonion.com/education/trend-of-violence-against-women-real-estate-agents/
- RAINN: rainn.org
- https://www.yahoo.com/lifestyle/man-bear-hypothetical-sparks-conversation-021728031.html
- https://www.elephantjournal.com/2024/05/man-vs-bear-why-some-women-are-choosing-the-bear-michelle-schafer/
- https://www.goodreads.com/work/quotes/1212277-the-gift-of-fear

Biography

Teacher, Analyst, Researcher, Author

Joanne Morin Correia

With a 2nd-degree Black Belt, served as an instructor at the National Academy of Self-Defense Education, teaching RAD Systems training in Basic (for Women, Men, and Kids) and advanced courses in Weapons and Keychain Defense.

At R+H Taekwondo (NH) and in Florida, conducted medical safety programs in First Aid and AED/CPR for children, women, and seniors.

Joanne was certified by Zumba Fitness, RAD Systems, and the American Red Cross, and is a proud member of the Black Belt Club in Moo Duk Kwan, a form of Taekwondo.

Quotes from our past students

"My "friends and I were so impressed and grateful for all we learned in our weekend class!" -"Family Doctor

"I recommend your self-defense course to women of all ages. I found your teaching style to be very easy to follow. You adjusted to meet the needs of the various ages in the class." - "e–istered Nurse

"Joanne and her son Jonathan provided us with priceless information and skills that could one day save our lives!" - Fitness Instructor

"I know a huge part of my trip's success was due to the training I received from you!" - AIDs Clinic Volunteer, South Africa.

Other Books

The US is Dangerous for Women

Available in eBook/Hard Copy

www.commonsensesafetyclasses.com

www.ingramcontent.com/pod-product-compliance
Lightning Source LLC
Chambersburg PA
CBHW070624030426
42337CB00020B/3902